Bliss

Unlocking the Secrets to Ultimate Happiness and Fulfillment: A Comprehensive Guide to Achieving Bliss in Every Aspect of Your Life - From Mastering Your Mindset to Cultivating Meaningful Relationships and Creating a Purposeful Life

Lance P. Richards

Bliss: Unlocking the Secrets to Ultimate Happiness and Fulfillment: A Comprehensive Guide to Achieving Bliss in Every Aspect of Your Life - From Mastering Your Mindset to Cultivating Meaningful Relationships and Creating a Purposeful Life

Table of Contents

01: Introduction: What is Bliss and Why is it Important?

Bliss: Unlocking the Secrets to Ultimate Happiness and Fulfillment is a comprehensive guide to achieving bliss in every aspect of your life. In this book, we will explore the different facets of life that contribute to our overall sense of happiness and fulfillment, and provide practical tips and strategies for cultivating a life of bliss.

But before we delve into the nitty-gritty of achieving bliss, let's first define what we mean by this term. Bliss is often used interchangeably with happiness, but it goes beyond just feeling good or experiencing pleasure. Bliss is a state of being in which we feel deeply content, satisfied, and fulfilled, regardless of our circumstances. It is a profound sense of inner peace, joy, and harmony that comes from living a life aligned with our deepest values and aspirations.

Bliss is not just a fleeting emotion or temporary high. It is a sustained state of being that arises from a combination of factors, including our mindset, our relationships, our health, our work, and our sense of purpose. When all these factors are in alignment, we experience a sense of wholeness and completeness that is greater than the sum of its parts.

01: INTRODUCTION: WHAT IS BLISS AND WHY IS IT IMPORTANT?

Why is Bliss Important?

Many people live their lives in a constant state of stress, anxiety, and dissatisfaction. They may have successful careers, loving relationships, and all the material comforts they could ask for, but still feel like something is missing. This is because they have not tapped into the deeper wellspring of joy and fulfillment that comes from living a life of purpose and meaning.

Bliss is important because it is the foundation of a fulfilling life. When we experience bliss, we are more resilient in the face of challenges, more creative in our work, and more loving and compassionate in our relationships. We are also more likely to take care of our physical, emotional, and spiritual health, which further enhances our sense of well-being.

Bliss is not just important for our individual well-being, but also for the greater good of society. When we are happy and fulfilled, we are more likely to contribute positively to our communities and the world around us. We are more likely to be kind, generous, and compassionate, and to work towards creating a better world for ourselves and future gen-

01: INTRODUCTION: WHAT IS BLISS AND WHY IS IT IMPORTANT?

erations.

The Path to Bliss

Bliss is not something that can be achieved overnight or through a quick fix. It requires a sustained effort to cultivate a life that is aligned with our deepest values and aspirations. This involves:

Mastering your mindset: Our thoughts and beliefs have a powerful impact on our emotions and actions. To cultivate bliss, we must learn to shift our mindset from one of scarcity and fear to one of abundance and possibility. This means letting go of limiting beliefs, cultivating a growth mindset, and practicing gratitude and mindfulness.

Cultivating meaningful relationships: We are social beings, and our relationships with others have a significant impact on our well-being. To cultivate bliss, we must invest in nurturing healthy, supportive, and fulfilling relationships with family, friends, and colleagues.

Prioritizing our health: Our physical, emotional, and spiritual health are interconnected, and neglecting any one of these areas can undermine our sense of well-being. To cultivate bliss, we must prioritize our health by eating well, exercising regularly, getting enough rest, managing stress, and cultivating practices that promote inner peace and connection.

Finding purpose and meaning: We all have a deep-seated need to feel like our lives have meaning and purpose. To cultivate bliss, we must identify our core values and passions, and align our work and activities with these values. This may involve making changes in our career or lifestyle, but the rewards of living a purpose-driven life are immeasurable.

In this book, we will explore each of these areas in detail, and provide practical tips and strategies for how you can cultivate bliss in your own life. We will draw on the latest research in psychology, neuroscience, and spirituality, as well as insights from experts and thought leaders in these fields.

We will also provide exercises and activities to help you apply these strategies in your own life, so that you can begin to experience greater levels of happiness and fulfillment right away. Whether you are struggling with stress, anxiety, or burnout, or simply looking to deepen your sense of well-being and purpose, this book will provide you with the tools and inspiration you need to create a life of bliss.

Throughout the book, we will also hear from individuals who have successfully cultivated bliss in their own lives. We will learn from their experiences and insights, and see how they have transformed their lives by aligning their mindset, relationships, health, and purpose with their deepest values and aspirations.

Ultimately, the path to bliss is a personal journey, and there is no one-size-fits-all formula for achieving it. But by following the principles and strategies outlined in this book, you can create a roadmap for your own journey towards greater happiness, fulfillment, and purpose.

So, whether you are just starting out on your journey or are already well on your way, I invite you to join me on this quest for bliss. Let's unlock the secrets to ultimate happiness and fulfillment, and create lives that are truly worth living.

01: INTRODUCTION: WHAT IS BLISS AND WHY IS IT IMPORTANT?

and strategies for how you can cultivate bliss in your own life. We will draw on the latest research in psychology, neuroscience, and spirituality, as well as insights from experts and thought leaders in these fields.

We will also provide exercises and activities to help you apply these strategies in your own life, so that you can begin to experience greater levels of happiness and fulfillment right away. Whether you are struggling with stress, anxiety, or burnout, or simply looking to deepen your sense of well-being and purpose, this book will provide you with the tools and inspiration you need to create a life of bliss.

Throughout the book, we will also hear from individuals who have successfully cultivated bliss in their own lives. We will learn from their experiences and insights, and see how they have transformed their lives by aligning their mindset, relationships, health, and purpose with their deepest values and aspirations.

Ultimately, the path to bliss is a personal journey, and there is no one-size-fits-all formula for achieving it. But by following the principles and strategies outlined in this book, you can create a roadmap for your own journey towards greater

01: INTRODUCTION: WHAT IS BLISS AND WHY IS IT IMPORTANT?

happiness, fulfillment, and purpose.

So, whether you are just starting out on your journey or are already well on your way, I invite you to join me on this quest for bliss. Let's unlock the secrets to ultimate happiness and fulfillment, and create lives that are truly worth living.

02: The Science of Happiness: Understanding the Psychology Behind Bliss

The pursuit of happiness is a universal goal, one that we all strive for in our lives. But what is happiness, really? Is it a fleeting emotion, or a sustained state of being? And how can we achieve it? The science of happiness, or positive psychology, seeks to answer these questions by examining the psychological factors that contribute to happiness and well-being. In this chapter, we will explore the key concepts and research findings of positive psychology, and learn how to apply them to our own lives in order to achieve greater happiness and fulfillment.

The Foundation of Positive Psychology

Positive psychology is a relatively new field of psychology, having emerged in the late 1990s as a response to the prevailing focus on pathology and dysfunction in traditional psychology. Instead of studying mental illness and negative states of mind, positive psychology seeks to understand the factors that contribute to positive states of mind, such as happiness, well-being, and flourishing.

02: THE SCIENCE OF HAPPINESS: UNDERSTANDING THE PSYCHOLOGY BEHIND BLISS

One of the key figures in the development of positive psychology is Martin Seligman, who outlined the field's basic tenets in his book, "Authentic Happiness." Seligman proposed that happiness and well-being can be achieved through three main components: positive emotions, engagement, and meaning. Positive emotions refer to feelings of pleasure and enjoyment, such as joy, contentment, and gratitude. Engagement refers to being fully absorbed in an activity, whether it's work, hobbies, or social interactions. And meaning refers to a sense of purpose and connection to something greater than oneself, such as a cause, a community, or a spiritual belief.

Research in Positive Psychology

Since its inception, positive psychology has generated a wealth of research on the factors that contribute to happiness and well-being. Some of the key findings include:

Positive emotions are associated with greater well-being: Studies have shown that people who experience more positive emotions, such as joy, gratitude, and contentment, report higher levels of life satisfaction and lower levels of depression and anxiety.

02: THE SCIENCE OF HAPPINESS: UNDERSTANDING THE PSYCHOLOGY BEHIND BLISS

Gratitude is a powerful predictor of happiness: People who regularly practice gratitude, whether through journaling or other activities, report greater happiness and well-being than those who do not.

Relationships are crucial for happiness: Strong social connections, whether with family, friends, or romantic partners, are consistently linked to greater happiness and well-being.

Meaning and purpose are essential for well-being: People who have a strong sense of meaning and purpose in their lives, whether through work, hobbies, or other pursuits, report greater happiness and fulfillment.

Mindfulness can increase well-being: Mindfulness practices, such as meditation, have been shown to reduce stress, improve mood, and increase overall well-being.

Applying Positive Psychology to Your Life

Now that we've explored some of the key concepts and research findings in positive psychology, let's take a closer look at how we can apply these ideas to our own lives in order to achieve greater happiness and fulfillment.

Practice gratitude: One of the simplest and most effective ways to increase happiness is to practice gratitude. Try keeping a gratitude journal, where you write down three things you're grateful for each day. Or make a habit of expressing gratitude to the people in your life who you appreciate.

Build strong relationships: Relationships are a crucial factor in happiness and well-being. Make time for the people in your life who matter most to you, and prioritize nurturing those relationships. Whether it's scheduling regular date nights with your partner, calling your parents once a week, or meeting up with friends for a coffee or a walk, make an effort to stay connected.

Find meaning and purpose: Having a sense of meaning and purpose in your life is essential for happiness and fulfillment. Think about what matters most to you, whether it's your career, your hobbies, your family, or your community. How can you use your skills and talents to make a positive impact on the world around you? How can you contribute to something greater than yourself? Reflecting on these questions can help you identify your purpose and find greater fulfillment in your daily life.

Practice mindfulness: Mindfulness practices, such as meditation, can help you cultivate a greater sense of awareness and presence in the present moment. This can reduce stress and anxiety, improve mood, and increase overall well-being. Start by setting aside just a few minutes each day to practice mindfulness, whether through guided meditations, deep breathing exercises, or simply taking a few moments to observe your thoughts and emotions without judgment.

Pursue hobbies and interests: Engaging in activities that you enjoy and are passionate about is a key factor in happiness and well-being. Whether it's playing a musical instrument, painting, hiking, or cooking, make time for the hobbies and interests that bring you joy and fulfillment. Not only will this help you feel happier and more fulfilled in the present moment, but it can also contribute to a greater sense of purpose and meaning in your life.

Cultivate positive relationships with yourself: Finally, it's important to remember that happiness and well-being begin with a positive relationship with yourself. Treat yourself with kindness, compassion, and forgiveness, and make self-care a priority. Whether it's taking time to exercise, getting enough sleep, or engaging in activities that bring you joy, prioritize your own well-being and happiness.

In conclusion, the science of happiness, or positive psychology, offers a wealth of insights and strategies for achieving greater happiness and fulfillment in our lives. By focusing on cultivating positive emotions, engagement, and meaning, as well as building strong relationships and practicing mindfulness, we can unlock the secrets to ultimate happiness and fulfillment. Remember, happiness is not a destination, but a journey that requires ongoing effort and commitment. But by applying the principles of positive psychology to our daily lives, we can all achieve greater happiness and fulfillment, one step at a time.

03: The Power of Positive Thinking: How to Master Your Mindset for a Blissful Life

Introduction:

Have you ever noticed how some people seem to effortlessly radiate happiness, positivity, and success, while others struggle to find even a glimmer of joy in their lives? The secret to their happiness and success lies in their mindset. Your thoughts, beliefs, and attitudes shape your reality, and the way you view the world around you can either propel you towards success or hold you back from achieving your goals.

In this chapter, we will explore the power of positive thinking and how it can transform your life, allowing you to experience greater happiness, fulfillment, and success in all areas of your life. From mastering your thoughts to cultivating gratitude and developing a growth mindset, we will cover the key principles of positive thinking and how to apply them to your life.

Part 1: Mastering Your Thoughts

03: THE POWER OF POSITIVE THINKING: HOW TO MASTER YOUR MINDSET FOR A BLISSFUL LIFE

The first step to cultivating a positive mindset is to master your thoughts. The way you think and talk to yourself has a powerful impact on your emotions and behavior. Negative self-talk and limiting beliefs can create a self-fulfilling prophecy, while positive self-talk and empowering beliefs can inspire you to take action and achieve your goals.

To master your thoughts, start by paying attention to the way you talk to yourself. Notice any negative self-talk or limiting beliefs that may be holding you back, and challenge them. Ask yourself, "Is this thought true? Is it helpful? Does it serve me?" If the answer is no, replace the negative thought with a positive one. For example, instead of thinking "I'm not good enough," try "I am capable and deserving of success."

Another powerful tool for mastering your thoughts is visualization. Visualization is a technique used by many successful athletes, entrepreneurs, and performers to achieve their goals. Simply close your eyes and imagine yourself achieving your desired outcome in vivid detail. Visualize the sights, sounds, and feelings associated with your success. By repeatedly visualizing your success, you are sending a powerful message to your subconscious mind that you are capable of achieving your goals.

Part 2: Cultivating Gratitude

Gratitude is the practice of focusing on the good in your life and expressing appreciation for it. When you cultivate gratitude, you shift your focus from what you lack to what you have, and this shift in perspective can have a powerful impact on your happiness and well-being.

To cultivate gratitude, start by keeping a gratitude journal. Each day, write down three things you are grateful for. They can be as simple as a sunny day or a cup of coffee, or as profound as a loving relationship or a meaningful accomplishment. By focusing on the good in your life, you are training your brain to notice and appreciate the positive aspects of your life.

Another powerful tool for cultivating gratitude is to express appreciation to others. Take the time to thank someone who has helped you, or send a note of appreciation to a loved one. By expressing gratitude to others, you are not only spreading positivity and kindness, but you are also reinforcing your own sense of gratitude and well-being.

Part 3: Developing a Growth Mindset

A growth mindset is the belief that your abilities and intelligence can be developed through effort and perseverance. This mindset is associated with greater resilience, creativity, and achievement, as it encourages you to embrace challenges and view failure as a learning opportunity.

To develop a growth mindset, start by reframing your beliefs about intelligence and talent. Instead of believing that you are born with a fixed level of intelligence or talent, believe that your abilities can be developed through practice and effort. Embrace challenges as opportunities to learn and grow, and view failures as stepping stones to success.

Another powerful tool for developing a growth mindset is to practice self-compassion. Treat yourself with the same kindness and understanding that you would offer to a friend. Recognize that setbacks and failures are a natural part of the learning process and that it's okay to make mistakes. By being kind and compassionate to yourself, you are creating a supportive and nurturing environment for growth and development.

Part 4: Surrounding Yourself with Positive Influences

The people you surround yourself with can have a powerful impact on your mindset and your life. Negative people and toxic relationships can drain your energy and hold you back from achieving your goals, while positive people and supportive relationships can inspire you and lift you up.

To surround yourself with positive influences, start by identifying the people in your life who bring you joy, support, and encouragement. Spend more time with these people and nurture these relationships. On the other hand, identify the people in your life who drain your energy or bring negativity into your life, and limit your interactions with them or cut them out of your life altogether.

Another powerful tool for surrounding yourself with positive influences is to seek out mentors and role models who inspire you. Look for people who have achieved success in the areas you are interested in and learn from their experiences and wisdom. By surrounding yourself with positive influences, you are creating a supportive and empowering environment for growth and success.

Conclusion:

Cultivating a positive mindset is not always easy, but the rewards are well worth the effort. By mastering your thoughts, cultivating gratitude, developing a growth mindset, and surrounding yourself with positive influences, you can unlock the secrets to ultimate happiness and fulfillment. Remember, happiness is not a destination, but a journey. It's not about achieving a certain goal or acquiring a certain possession, but about living a life filled with meaning, purpose, and joy. With the power of positive thinking, you can create the life of your dreams and experience true bliss in every aspect of your life.

04: Mindfulness and Meditation: Techniques for Cultivating Inner Peace and Joy

Introduction

In today's fast-paced world, it's easy to feel overwhelmed, stressed, and disconnected from ourselves. We often find ourselves running on autopilot, going through the motions without really being present in the moment. However, cultivating mindfulness and practicing meditation can help us tap into a deeper sense of inner peace, joy, and fulfillment. In this chapter, we'll explore the benefits of mindfulness and meditation, different techniques for practicing them, and how to incorporate them into your daily life.

The Benefits of Mindfulness and Meditation

Mindfulness and meditation have been shown to have a wide range of benefits for both physical and mental health. Here are just a few:

Reduced stress and anxiety: Mindfulness and meditation can help reduce stress and anxiety by helping us focus on the present moment instead of worrying about the future or ruminating on the past.

Improved mental clarity and focus: Regular meditation practice can improve mental clarity, focus, and concentration, which can lead to increased productivity and creativity.

Increased self-awareness: By cultivating mindfulness, we become more aware of our thoughts, emotions, and physical sensations, which can help us better understand ourselves and our patterns of behavior.

Improved relationships: Mindfulness and meditation can help us cultivate more empathy and compassion for ourselves and others, leading to stronger and more meaningful relationships.

Improved physical health: Regular meditation practice has been linked to lower blood pressure, improved sleep, and reduced inflammation, among other physical health benefits.

Different Techniques for Mindfulness and Meditation

There are many different techniques for practicing mindfulness and meditation, and what works best for you may depend on your preferences, lifestyle, and goals. Here are a few different techniques to consider:

Mindful breathing: Mindful breathing involves simply paying attention to your breath as it goes in and out. You can do this anywhere, anytime, and it's a great way to ground yourself in the present moment.

Body scan: A body scan involves focusing your attention on different parts of your body, one at a time, and noticing any physical sensations that arise. This can help you become more aware of any tension or discomfort in your body and release it.

Loving-kindness meditation: Loving-kindness meditation involves sending positive thoughts and well-wishes to yourself and others. This can help cultivate a sense of empathy and compassion for yourself and others.

Walking meditation: Walking meditation involves paying attention to your body and surroundings as you walk, rather than being lost in your thoughts. It's a great way to get some exercise and practice mindfulness at the same time.

Mantra meditation: Mantra meditation involves repeating a word, phrase, or sound to help focus your attention and quiet your mind. This can be especially helpful if you find it difficult to quiet your mind on your own.

Incorporating Mindfulness and Meditation into Your Daily Life

While it's great to set aside time specifically for mindfulness and meditation practice, it's also important to try to incorporate these practices into your daily life. Here are a few ways to do that:

Mindful eating: Pay attention to the taste, texture, and smell of your food as you eat, rather than eating mindlessly while doing other things.

Mindful walking: Instead of being lost in thought while walking, try to pay attention to your surroundings and the sensations in your body as you move.

Mindful listening: When someone is talking to you, try to really listen to what they're saying and be fully present in the conversation, rather than thinking about other things.

04: MINDFULNESS AND MEDITATION: TECHNIQUES FOR CULTIVATING INNER PEACE AND JOY

Mindful driving: Pay attention to your breath and the sensations in your body as you drive, rather than getting lost in thought or reacting to other drivers.

Mindful cleaning: When cleaning your home, try to focus your attention on the task at hand and the sensations in your body as you move. Notice the way the cleaning supplies smell, the way the surfaces feel under your hands, and the way your body feels as you move around.

Mindful technology use: Try to be more mindful of your technology use by setting aside specific times for checking emails and social media rather than constantly checking throughout the day. When you do use technology, try to be fully present and engaged rather than multitasking or getting lost in mindless scrolling.

Mindful self-care: Take time each day for self-care activities like yoga, stretching, or taking a bath. As you engage in these activities, try to be fully present in the moment and focus on the sensations in your body.

By incorporating mindfulness and meditation into your daily life, you can start to cultivate a greater sense of inner peace and joy that will spill over into every aspect of your life.

Overcoming Obstacles to Mindfulness and Meditation

While mindfulness and meditation can have many benefits, they can also be challenging to practice consistently. Here are a few common obstacles to mindfulness and meditation and some strategies for overcoming them:

Lack of time: If you feel like you don't have enough time to practice mindfulness and meditation, start with just a few minutes a day and gradually work your way up to longer periods of time. You can also try to incorporate mindfulness into activities you're already doing, like washing dishes or taking a walk.

Difficulty quieting the mind: If you find it difficult to quiet your mind during meditation, try using a guided meditation app or following a mantra meditation practice. You can also try simply observing your thoughts without getting caught up in them or imagining them as clouds passing by in the sky.

Impatience or frustration: If you feel impatient or frustrated during meditation, try to be gentle with yourself and remind yourself that it's a practice. You can also try focusing on the sensations in your body or bringing your attention back to your breath when you get distracted.

Discomfort or pain: If you experience discomfort or pain during meditation, try adjusting your posture or sitting on a cushion. You can also try a different meditation technique or take a break if needed.

Conclusion

Incorporating mindfulness and meditation into your life can have a profound impact on your overall sense of well-being and happiness. By practicing mindfulness and meditation, you can cultivate a greater sense of inner peace, joy, and ful-fillment, and improve your relationships, productivity, and physical health. While it may take some time and practice to develop these skills, the benefits are well worth the effort. So why not start today?

05: Gratitude and Appreciation: The Key to Unlocking the Fullness of Life

Gratitude and appreciation are the keys to unlocking the fullness of life. When we cultivate an attitude of gratitude and learn to appreciate the many blessings in our lives, we become happier, more content, and more fulfilled. This chapter will explore the importance of gratitude and appreciation, and provide practical tips and strategies for cultivating these qualities in your life.

The Power of Gratitude

Gratitude is a powerful emotion that has the ability to transform our lives. When we focus on what we are grateful for, we shift our attention away from what we lack or what we perceive as negative in our lives. Instead, we focus on the good things in our lives and the many blessings we have been given. This shift in focus has a profound effect on our overall happiness and well-being.

Research has shown that practicing gratitude can have numerous benefits, including improved physical health, increased happiness and life satisfaction, and reduced feelings of depression and anxiety. Studies have also shown that people who regularly practice gratitude are more likely to be optimistic, have stronger relationships, and are more resilient in the face of adversity.

How to Cultivate Gratitude

Cultivating gratitude is a simple practice that anyone can do, regardless of their circumstances. Here are some practical tips for cultivating gratitude in your life:

Keep a gratitude journal: Write down three things you are grateful for each day. This simple practice can help you focus on the good things in your life and shift your attention away from negativity.

Practice mindfulness: Take time each day to focus on the present moment and pay attention to the beauty and wonder around you. Notice the small things in your life that you may have taken for granted, such as a beautiful sunset or a kind word from a friend.

Say thank you: Take the time to express your gratitude to others. Whether it's a simple thank you to a cashier or a heartfelt expression of gratitude to a loved one, expressing your appreciation can have a positive impact on both you and the person you are thanking.

Focus on the positive: Instead of dwelling on the negative aspects of your life, try to focus on the positive. Look for the good in every situation and try to find the silver lining in difficult circumstances.

Practice gratitude in difficult times: When you are facing challenging times, it can be difficult to feel grateful. However, this is often when practicing gratitude is most important. Take time to focus on the things in your life that are going well, no matter how small they may seem.

The Importance of Appreciation

Appreciation is another important aspect of cultivating happiness and fulfillment in our lives. When we appreciate the people, things, and experiences in our lives, we cultivate a sense of abundance and gratitude that can have a powerful impact on our overall well-being.

Appreciation also helps us cultivate deeper, more meaningful relationships with the people in our lives. When we take the time to appreciate others, we demonstrate that we value and care for them. This can lead to stronger, more fulfilling relationships that provide us with a sense of connection and belonging.

How to Cultivate Appreciation

Cultivating appreciation is a practice that requires mindfulness and intentionality. Here are some practical tips for cultivating appreciation in your life:

Notice the small things: Take time to notice the small things in your life that bring you joy and happiness. It could be a beautiful sunset, a warm cup of tea, or a kind word from a friend. When you notice these things, take a moment to appreciate them.

Express appreciation to others: Take time to express your appreciation to the people in your life. Whether it's a simple thank you or a heartfelt expression of gratitude, taking the time to appreciate others can have a powerful impact on your relationships.

05: GRATITUDE AND APPRECIATION: THE KEY TO UN-LOCKING THE FULLNESS OF LIFE

Focus on the present moment: When we are caught up in the busyness of life, it can be easy to overlook the many blessings in our lives. By focusing on the present moment and being fully present in the experiences we are having, we can cultivate a deeper appreciation for the people, things, and experiences in our lives.

Practice mindfulness: Mindfulness is a powerful practice that can help us cultivate appreciation in our lives. By being fully present and non-judgmental in our experiences, we can learn to appreciate the beauty and wonder in the world around us.

Practice gratitude and appreciation together: Gratitude and appreciation are interconnected practices that can reinforce one another. By practicing both gratitude and appreciation in your life, you can cultivate a deeper sense of contentment and fulfillment.

The Benefits of Gratitude and Appreciation

The benefits of gratitude and appreciation are numerous and far-reaching. By cultivating these qualities in your life, you can experience greater happiness, contentment, and fulfillment. Here are just a few of the many benefits of gratitude and appreciation:

Improved relationships: When we take the time to appreciate and express gratitude for the people in our lives, we cultivate deeper, more meaningful relationships that provide us with a sense of connection and belonging.

Increased happiness and life satisfaction: Research has shown that practicing gratitude and appreciation can lead to increased happiness and life satisfaction.

Improved physical health: Gratitude and appreciation have been linked to improved physical health, including a stronger immune system, lower blood pressure, and reduced symptoms of stress and anxiety.

Increased resilience: People who regularly practice gratitude and appreciation are more resilient in the face of adversity and are better able to bounce back from difficult experiences.

Increased success: Research has shown that people who practice gratitude and appreciation are more successful in their personal and professional lives.

In Conclusion

Gratitude and appreciation are powerful practices that have the ability to transform our lives. By cultivating an attitude of gratitude and learning to appreciate the many blessings in our lives, we can experience greater happiness, contentment, and fulfillment. Whether through keeping a gratitude journal, expressing appreciation to others, or simply focusing on the present moment, there are many practical ways to cultivate gratitude and appreciation in your life. By incorporating these practices into your daily routine, you can unlock the fullness of life and experience the true bliss that comes from living a life of gratitude and appreciation.

06: Joyful Movement: How Exercise and Movement Can Bring More Bliss to Your Life

Exercise and movement have always been associated with physical health and fitness. However, the benefits of regular exercise and movement go far beyond just physical health. Exercise and movement have a significant impact on mental health, emotional well-being, and overall happiness and fulfillment. In this chapter, we will explore the science behind the connection between exercise and happiness, and how you can incorporate joyful movement into your life to experience more bliss.

The Science of Exercise and Happiness

When we exercise, our bodies release endorphins, which are chemicals that create feelings of euphoria and happiness. Endorphins are natural painkillers, and they can reduce stress and anxiety, improve mood, and increase energy levels. This is why people often feel a sense of accomplishment and happiness after a workout.

But the benefits of exercise and movement go beyond just endorphins. Regular exercise has been linked to a lower risk of depression and anxiety, improved cognitive function, better sleep, and improved self-esteem. Exercise can also be a great way to reduce stress and improve overall mood.

The type of exercise you do can also have an impact on your mental health. Aerobic exercise, such as running, cycling, or swimming, has been shown to have the most significant impact on mental health. However, strength training and other forms of exercise can also be beneficial.

Incorporating Joyful Movement into Your Life

Exercise doesn't have to be a chore. In fact, the more you enjoy your exercise routine, the more likely you are to stick with it. Here are some tips for incorporating joyful movement into your life:

Find an activity you enjoy: Not everyone enjoys running or going to the gym. Find an activity that you enjoy, whether it's dancing, hiking, swimming, or playing a sport. When you enjoy the activity, you're more likely to look forward to it and feel a sense of fulfillment when you're done.

Make it social: Exercise doesn't have to be a solitary activity.

06: JOYFUL MOVEMENT: HOW EXERCISE AND MOVE-MENT CAN BRING MORE BLISS TO YOUR LIFE

Join a sports team, take a dance class, or go for a walk with a friend. When you exercise with others, you get the added benefit of social interaction, which can improve mood and reduce stress.

Mix it up: Doing the same exercise routine day after day can get boring. Mix it up by trying new activities or varying your routine. This can keep your exercise routine fresh and exciting, and prevent boredom.

Set achievable goals: Setting goals can give you a sense of purpose and direction. However, it's important to set achievable goals that are within your reach. This can give you a sense of accomplishment and motivation to continue.

Make it a habit: The more you exercise, the easier it becomes. Make exercise a habit by scheduling it into your day and sticking to a routine. This can make it easier to stick with it, even on days when you don't feel like it.

The Importance of Rest and Recovery

While exercise is essential for physical and mental health, it's also important to rest and recover. Overtraining can lead to burnout, injury, and other negative consequences. Here are some tips for incorporating rest and recovery into your exercise routine:

Listen to your body: Your body knows when it needs rest. If you're feeling tired or run down, take a day off from exercise or do a lighter workout.

Incorporate active recovery: Active recovery involves doing low-intensity exercise, such as walking or stretching, to help your body recover. This can be a great way to stay active while giving your body a break.

Get enough sleep: Sleep is essential for physical and mental health. Make sure you're getting enough sleep, especially on days when you exercise.

Fuel your body: Eating a healthy diet can help your body recover from exercise. Make sure you're eating enough protein to help repair and rebuild muscles, and consuming plenty of fruits and vegetables for important vitamins and minerals. It's also important to stay hydrated by drinking plenty of water throughout the day.

06: JOYFUL MOVEMENT: HOW EXERCISE AND MOVEMENT CAN BRING MORE BLISS TO YOUR LIFE

Take breaks: It's okay to take breaks from exercise. If you're feeling burnt out or unmotivated, take a few days or a week off from exercise. This can give your body and mind a chance to rest and recover, so you can come back to exercise feeling refreshed and energized.

Incorporating Movement into Your Daily Life

Exercise is just one way to incorporate movement into your life. There are many other ways to stay active throughout the day, even if you don't have time for a full workout. Here are some tips for incorporating movement into your daily life:

Take the stairs: Instead of taking the elevator, take the stairs. This can be a great way to get your heart rate up and incorporate some movement into your day.

Walk or bike to work: If you live close enough to work, consider walking or biking instead of driving. This can be a great way to get some exercise and fresh air before and after work.

Stand up and stretch: If you have a desk job, make sure

you're taking breaks to stand up and stretch throughout the day. This can help prevent stiffness and improve circulation.

Dance: Dancing is a fun and joyful way to incorporate movement into your day. Put on some music and dance around your living room, or take a dance class for a more structured workout.

Do household chores: Cleaning, cooking, and other household chores can be a great way to stay active. Vacuuming, mopping, and sweeping can all get your heart rate up, and cooking can involve lots of movement and standing.

Final Thoughts

Exercise and movement are essential for physical and mental health, and can be a great way to experience more bliss in your life. By finding activities you enjoy, incorporating social interaction, and setting achievable goals, you can make exercise a joyful and fulfilling part of your daily routine. And by incorporating movement into your daily life, even in small ways, you can stay active and improve your overall health and well-being. Remember to listen to your body, take breaks when you need them, and make rest and recovery a priority. With these tips, you can unlock the secrets to ultimate happiness and fulfillment through joyful movement.

07: Nourishing Your Body: The Connection Between Nutrition and Happiness

Introduction:

When it comes to achieving ultimate happiness and fulfillment in life, many factors come into play. One of the most important of these is taking care of your physical health, and the cornerstone of good physical health is proper nutrition. Nourishing your body with a healthy, balanced diet has a profound impact on your physical and mental well-being, and can help you to achieve greater levels of happiness and fulfillment in every aspect of your life.

In this chapter, we will explore the connection between nutrition and happiness, and provide you with practical tips and strategies for nourishing your body and achieving optimal health.

The Importance of Proper Nutrition:

Proper nutrition is essential for maintaining good health and well-being. It provides the body with the nutrients it needs to function properly, and helps to prevent a range of health problems, including obesity, diabetes, heart disease, and certain types of cancer.

In addition to its physical benefits, proper nutrition also has a profound impact on mental health and well-being. Studies have shown that a healthy, balanced diet can help to reduce the risk of depression and anxiety, and can even improve cognitive function and memory.

The Connection Between Nutrition and Happiness:

The connection between nutrition and happiness is a complex one, but it is clear that what we eat has a profound impact on our mood, energy levels, and overall well-being. When we consume a diet that is rich in whole, nutrient-dense foods, we are providing our bodies with the fuel and nutrients they need to function at their best.

By contrast, when we consume a diet that is high in processed, sugary, or fatty foods, we are putting ourselves at risk for a range of health problems, including obesity, diabetes, and heart disease. In addition to the physical risks, these types of foods can also have a negative impact on our mood and energy levels, leading to feelings of lethargy, irritability, and depression.

The Benefits of a Healthy, Balanced Diet:

A healthy, balanced diet is essential for achieving optimal health and well-being. Some of the key benefits of a healthy, balanced diet include:

Increased energy levels: When we consume a diet that is rich in whole, nutrient-dense foods, we provide our bodies with the fuel they need to function at their best. This can help to boost our energy levels and improve our overall productivity and performance.

Improved mental health: Studies have shown that a healthy, balanced diet can help to reduce the risk of depression and anxiety, and can even improve cognitive function and memory.

Weight management: A healthy, balanced diet can help to maintain a healthy weight, which is essential for reducing the risk of obesity, diabetes, and other chronic health problems.

Improved immune function: A diet that is rich in whole, nu-

07: NOURISHING YOUR BODY: THE CONNECTION BETWEEN NUTRITION AND HAPPINESS

trient-dense foods can help to boost our immune system and reduce the risk of illness and infection.

Better sleep: A healthy, balanced diet can help to improve our sleep quality, which is essential for maintaining good health and well-being.

Tips for Nourishing Your Body:

If you want to nourish your body and achieve optimal health and well-being, here are some practical tips and strategies to help you get started:

Eat a variety of nutrient-dense foods: Aim to consume a variety of fruits, vegetables, whole grains, lean proteins, and healthy fats. These foods provide your body with the essential nutrients it needs to function properly and thrive.

Avoid processed and sugary foods: Processed and sugary foods can wreak havoc on your mood and energy levels, and can contribute to a range of health problems. Aim to minimize your consumption of these types of foods, and instead focus on whole, nutrient-dense foods.

Stay hydrated: Drinking plenty of water is essential for

maintaining good health and well-being. Aim to drink at least eight glasses of water per day, and avoid sugary drinks and excessive amounts of caffeine, as these can lead to dehydration.

Practice mindful eating: Mindful eating involves paying close attention to your food, savoring each bite, and eating slowly and intentionally. This can help you to better appreciate your food, and may also help you to eat less and make healthier choices.

Plan ahead: Planning your meals ahead of time can help you to make healthier choices, and can also save you time and money. Try to set aside time each week to plan out your meals and snacks, and make a shopping list to ensure that you have all the ingredients you need.

Cook at home: Cooking at home allows you to control the ingredients that go into your meals, and can help you to make healthier choices. Try to cook as many meals at home as possible, and experiment with new recipes and ingredients to keep things interesting.

Take supplements if necessary: While a healthy, balanced

diet is the best way to get the nutrients your body needs, there may be times when you need to supplement your diet with vitamins or minerals. Consult with your doctor or a registered dietitian to determine if supplements are right for you.

Conclusion:

Nourishing your body with a healthy, balanced diet is essential for achieving optimal health and well-being. By consuming whole, nutrient-dense foods, staying hydrated, and practicing mindful eating, you can provide your body with the fuel and nutrients it needs to function at its best. Whether you are looking to improve your mental health, manage your weight, or simply feel better overall, making nutrition a priority is a key step in achieving ultimate happiness and fulfillment in every aspect of your life.

08: Sleep and Rest: The Importance of Sleep for a Blissful Life

Sleep and rest are crucial components of a healthy and blissful life. Unfortunately, in today's fast-paced world, many people sacrifice their sleep and rest in order to keep up with their busy schedules. However, this can lead to a multitude of negative consequences, including poor health, increased stress, and decreased productivity. In this chapter, we will explore the importance of sleep and rest, and provide practical tips for optimizing these essential components of a blissful life.

Why Sleep and Rest Are Important

Sleep is essential for the body and mind to function optimally. During sleep, the body repairs itself, and the brain consolidates memories and processes emotions. Lack of sleep can lead to a range of negative consequences, including reduced cognitive function, increased stress, and decreased immune function. Rest, on the other hand, allows the body and mind to recharge and rejuvenate, reducing stress and increasing overall well-being.

The Importance of Quality Sleep

08: SLEEP AND REST: THE IMPORTANCE OF SLEEP FOR A BLISSFUL LIFE

While it is important to get enough sleep, the quality of your sleep is just as important as the quantity. Quality sleep is characterized by several factors, including the duration, depth, and continuity of sleep. If you are not getting quality sleep, you may experience a range of negative consequences, including fatigue, irritability, and difficulty concentrating.

To optimize the quality of your sleep, it is important to establish a consistent sleep schedule and sleep environment. This means going to bed and waking up at the same time each day, avoiding caffeine and alcohol before bed, and creating a comfortable and dark sleep environment. Additionally, incorporating relaxation techniques such as meditation or deep breathing can help to calm the mind and promote restful sleep.

The Importance of Rest

While sleep is essential for the body and mind to function optimally, rest is just as important for overall well-being. Rest allows the body and mind to recharge and rejuvenate, reducing stress and increasing overall well-being. Rest can take many forms, including relaxation, meditation, and physical activity. By incorporating rest into your daily routine, you can reduce stress, increase productivity, and improve overall health.

Tips for Optimizing Sleep and Rest

If you are struggling to get enough quality sleep or rest, there are several tips and strategies you can implement to optimize these essential components of a blissful life. Some of these tips include:

– Establish a consistent sleep schedule and sleep environment. This means going to bed and waking up at the same time each day, avoiding caffeine and alcohol before bed, and creating a comfortable and dark sleep environment.

– Practice relaxation techniques such as meditation or deep breathing to calm the mind and promote restful sleep.

– Incorporate physical activity into your daily routine to promote rest and reduce stress.

– Take regular breaks throughout the day to rest and recharge.

08: SLEEP AND REST: THE IMPORTANCE OF SLEEP FOR A BLISSFUL LIFE

– Prioritize self-care activities such as massage, acupuncture, or yoga to reduce stress and promote rest and relaxation.

– Create a calming bedtime routine to help signal to your body that it is time to sleep.

– Avoid using electronic devices before bed, as the blue light emitted by these devices can interfere with sleep.

– Consider using natural sleep aids such as melatonin or valerian root to promote restful sleep.

Incorporating these tips and strategies into your daily routine can help you to optimize sleep and rest, leading to improved overall well-being and a more blissful life.

In conclusion, sleep and rest are essential components of a healthy and blissful life. By prioritizing these essential components, you can reduce stress, increase productivity, and improve overall well-being. So, make sure to establish a consistent sleep schedule and sleep environment, practice relaxation techniques, incorporate physical activity into your daily routine, and prioritize self-care activities to op-

08: SLEEP AND REST: THE IMPORTANCE OF SLEEP FOR A BLISSFUL LIFE

timize sleep and rest and unlock the secrets to ultimate happiness and fulfillment.

09: Mindful Breathing: How Breathwork Can Help You Achieve Greater Bliss

As you sit quietly with your eyes closed, take a deep breath in through your nose and slowly exhale through your mouth. Feel the coolness of the air as it enters your nostrils and the warmth of your breath as it exits your lips. Focus on the sensation of your breath as it moves in and out of your body, bringing a sense of calm and relaxation with each inhale and exhale.

This simple exercise is an example of mindful breathing, a powerful technique that has been used for centuries to promote relaxation, reduce stress, and improve overall well-being. Mindful breathing involves paying attention to your breath in a non-judgmental way, without trying to control it or change it in any way.

In recent years, the benefits of mindful breathing have been supported by scientific research. Studies have shown that regular practice of mindful breathing can lower blood pressure, reduce symptoms of anxiety and depression, and improve immune function. It can also help you sleep better, increase your focus and productivity, and enhance your overall sense of happiness and well-being.

But what exactly is mindful breathing, and how can you incorporate it into your daily life? In this chapter, we will explore the practice of breathwork and the many ways it can help you achieve greater bliss in every aspect of your life.

The Basics of Mindful Breathing

At its core, mindful breathing is a form of meditation that involves paying attention to your breath in a non-judgmental way. This means simply observing your breath as it comes in and out of your body, without trying to change it or control it in any way.

To practice mindful breathing, find a quiet place where you can sit comfortably and focus on your breath. Close your eyes and take a deep breath in through your nose, filling your lungs with air. Hold your breath for a few seconds, and then slowly exhale through your mouth, feeling the tension release from your body.

As you continue to breathe in this way, focus on the sensation of your breath moving in and out of your body. Notice the rise and fall of your chest, the expansion and contraction of your lungs, and the movement of your diaphragm. If your mind wanders, gently bring your attention back to your breath, without judgment or criticism.

Mindful breathing can be practiced anywhere, at any time, and can be adapted to suit your needs and preferences. You can practice it for a few minutes each day, or for longer periods of time if you prefer. Some people find it helpful to incorporate mindful breathing into their daily routine, such as before bed or during their lunch break.

Benefits of Mindful Breathing

The benefits of mindful breathing are numerous and far-reaching. Here are just a few of the ways that regular practice of breathwork can help you achieve greater bliss in your life:

Reduced stress and anxiety: Mindful breathing has been shown to lower levels of cortisol, a hormone that is produced in response to stress. This can help reduce feelings of anxiety and promote a sense of calm and relaxation.

09: MINDFUL BREATHING: HOW BREATHWORK CAN HELP YOU ACHIEVE GREATER BLISS

Improved focus and productivity: By focusing on your breath, you can improve your ability to concentrate and stay focused on the task at hand. This can help you be more productive and efficient in your daily life.

Better sleep: Mindful breathing can help calm your mind and body, making it easier to fall asleep and stay asleep throughout the night.

Enhanced immune function: Studies have shown that regular practice of breathwork can boost immune function, helping you stay healthy and ward off illness.

Greater self-awareness: Mindful breathing can help you become more aware of your thoughts, emotions, and physical sensations. This can help you identify areas of your life that may be causing stress or discomfort, and make positive changes to improve your overall well-being.

Improved emotional regulation: Mindful breathing can help you regulate your emotions, making it easier to manage difficult feelings and respond to situations in a more balanced and effective way.

09: MINDFUL BREATHING: HOW BREATHWORK CAN HELP YOU ACHIEVE GREATER BLISS

Greater sense of connection: By focusing on your breath, you can become more present and attuned to the world around you, fostering a greater sense of connection to yourself, others, and the natural world.

Increased sense of happiness and well-being: Regular practice of mindful breathing has been shown to increase feelings of happiness and well-being, helping you experience greater joy and fulfillment in your life.

Incorporating Mindful Breathing into Your Daily Life

Now that you understand the benefits of mindful breathing, you may be wondering how to incorporate this practice into your daily life. Here are a few tips to help you get started:

Set aside time each day to practice: Whether it's first thing in the morning, during your lunch break, or before bed, try to set aside a few minutes each day to practice mindful breathing.

Find a quiet, comfortable place to practice: Choose a quiet, comfortable place where you won't be disturbed, and where you can sit comfortably with your back straight and your feet flat on the floor.

Set an intention for your practice: Before you begin, set an intention for your practice. This could be to reduce stress, improve focus, or simply to cultivate a sense of calm and relaxation.

Focus on your breath: As you begin to practice, focus on the sensation of your breath moving in and out of your body. If your mind wanders, gently bring your attention back to your breath, without judgment or criticism.

Practice regularly: Like any skill, mindful breathing takes practice. Try to practice regularly, even if it's just for a few minutes each day, to experience the full benefits of this powerful technique.

In addition to formal practice, there are many ways to incorporate mindful breathing into your daily life. You can use breathwork to help calm your mind and reduce stress in stressful situations, or to improve your focus and productivity when working on a task. You can also use mindful breathing to enhance your yoga or meditation practice, or to promote a sense of calm and relaxation before bed.

09: MINDFUL BREATHING: HOW BREATHWORK CAN HELP YOU ACHIEVE GREATER BLISS

Conclusion

Mindful breathing is a powerful tool that can help you achieve greater bliss in every aspect of your life. By paying attention to your breath in a non-judgmental way, you can reduce stress and anxiety, improve focus and productivity, and enhance your overall sense of well-being.

Whether you choose to practice mindful breathing formally, through meditation or yoga, or informally, throughout your daily life, this technique can have a profound impact on your physical, emotional, and spiritual health. So take a deep breath, and begin your journey towards greater bliss and fulfillment today.

10: Creativity and Self-Expression: The Role of Art and Creativity in Finding Happiness

The pursuit of happiness is a never-ending journey that requires a holistic approach. It's a quest that requires one to delve deep within themselves, explore their innermost desires, and express their true selves. Creativity and self-expression are powerful tools that help unlock the secrets to ultimate happiness and fulfillment. They play a critical role in shaping our perspective and outlook on life, allowing us to connect with our innermost selves and find joy in our everyday lives.

Art has been a powerful tool for self-expression throughout human history. From ancient cave paintings to modern-day masterpieces, art has always been a medium for expressing our deepest emotions and thoughts. Art allows us to connect with our emotions, communicate our feelings, and explore our imaginations. It gives us a platform to express ourselves without fear of judgment or reprisal. It allows us to connect with ourselves and others on a deeper level, fostering empathy and understanding.

10: CREATIVITY AND SELF-EXPRESSION: THE ROLE OF ART AND CREATIVITY IN FINDING HAPPINESS

The creative process is a journey of self-discovery. It's a path that allows us to explore our innermost desires, unleash our imagination, and find our unique voice. Creativity helps us tap into our innate talents and abilities, giving us a sense of purpose and fulfillment. When we engage in creative activities, we enter a state of flow, where time seems to stand still, and we lose ourselves in the moment. This state of flow is highly rewarding and can lead to a sense of accomplishment and satisfaction.

Artistic expression can take many forms, including painting, drawing, writing, sculpting, singing, dancing, and acting. Whatever form it takes, the creative process is a powerful tool for personal growth and transformation. When we create something, we bring a part of ourselves into existence. We leave a mark on the world, and that sense of accomplishment can be highly rewarding.

Creativity and self-expression are not just for artists and performers. Everyone has the ability to be creative and express themselves in their unique way. Whether it's cooking a delicious meal, gardening, or designing a website, there are endless ways to tap into our creativity and express ourselves. The key is to find what works for us and make time for it in our busy lives.

Incorporating creativity and self-expression into our daily lives can have a significant impact on our overall happiness and well-being. It allows us to connect with ourselves and others, reducing stress, anxiety, and depression. It can also help us develop a positive mindset, increasing our resilience and ability to cope with life's challenges.

In conclusion, creativity and self-expression are powerful tools that help unlock the secrets to ultimate happiness and fulfillment. By engaging in creative activities and finding ways to express ourselves, we tap into our innate talents and abilities, foster empathy and understanding, and connect with ourselves and others on a deeper level. Whether it's through art, writing, cooking, or any other form of creative expression, the key is to find what works for us and make time for it in our lives. By doing so, we can unlock the door to a life filled with bliss and meaning.

11: The Importance of Play: How Fun and Play Can Enhance Your Bliss

Introduction:

When was the last time you played like a child, without any worry or fear of judgment? Do you remember the pure joy and happiness that filled your heart during those moments? Playing is not just for children; it's an essential aspect of our well-being and happiness as adults. In fact, play can significantly impact our physical, mental, and emotional health, enhancing our overall sense of bliss and fulfillment.

In this chapter, we'll explore the importance of play, how it can improve our lives, and how to incorporate more play into our daily routines.

Section 1: The Benefits of Play

1.1 Play Enhances Creativity

When we engage in play, we open up our minds to new ideas and ways of thinking. Play encourages us to think outside the box and find creative solutions to problems. Studies have shown that individuals who engage in play have increased levels of creativity and innovation.

1.2 Play Reduces Stress and Anxiety

Play can also help us relax and reduce stress and anxiety. When we engage in play, we release endorphins, which are natural feel-good chemicals that boost our mood and decrease stress levels. Engaging in play can also help us forget about our problems temporarily, providing us with a mental break and allowing us to recharge our batteries.

1.3 Play Improves Relationships

When we play with others, we build stronger bonds and deeper connections. Play encourages social interaction, which can lead to improved communication skills, increased empathy, and a greater sense of belonging. Playing with our romantic partners can also help us deepen our intimacy and strengthen our emotional connection.

1.4 Play Boosts Physical Health

Engaging in physical play, such as sports or outdoor activities, can improve our physical health. Play can help us maintain a healthy weight, improve our cardiovascular health, and strengthen our muscles and bones. Physical play can also help us get better sleep and increase our energy levels.

Section 2: How to Incorporate More Play into Your Life

2.1 Find Your Play Personality

Everyone has a unique play personality, which refers to the types of activities and games that they enjoy most. Some people prefer physical play, while others enjoy creative or social play. Discovering your play personality can help you identify the types of activities that will bring you the most joy and fulfillment.

2.2 Make Time for Play

One of the biggest challenges of incorporating play into our lives is finding the time to do so. However, it's essential to prioritize playtime just as we would any other important aspect of our lives. Set aside a specific time each day or week to engage in play, and treat it as non-negotiable time on your schedule.

2.3 Try New Activities

11: THE IMPORTANCE OF PLAY: HOW FUN AND PLAY CAN ENHANCE YOUR BLISS

Trying new activities can help us discover new passions and interests. Don't be afraid to step outside of your comfort zone and try something new. Sign up for a dance class, join a sports league, or take an art class. The possibilities are endless!

2.4 Play with Others

Playing with others can enhance the fun and enjoyment of play. Invite friends or family members to join you in your playtime activities. You can also join social groups or clubs centered around your favorite types of play.

2.5 Bring Play into Your Work

Incorporating play into our work can help us be more productive and creative. Find ways to add elements of play into your workday, such as taking a quick break to play a game, incorporating playful elements into your workspace, or engaging in creative brainstorming sessions with colleagues.

Conclusion:

Incorporating more play into our lives can significantly impact our overall sense of bliss and fulfillment. Whether it's engaging in physical play, creative play, or social play, finding ways to incorporate play into our daily routines can help us reduce stress and anxiety, boost our creativity, improve our relationships, and enhance our physical health. By prioritizing playtime and discovering our unique play personalities, we can find joy and happiness in the activities that bring us the most fulfillment.

It's easy to get caught up in the demands of daily life and forget about the importance of play. But by incorporating more play into our lives, we can achieve a more balanced and fulfilling lifestyle. So, let's make time for play, try new activities, and invite others to join us in the fun. Let's rediscover the pure joy and happiness of childhood and unlock the secrets to ultimate happiness and fulfillment.

12: Finding Purpose: The Significance of Meaning and Purpose in a Blissful Life

As humans, we all desire to lead fulfilling and meaningful lives, to feel that our existence matters and that we have a purpose. Without a sense of purpose, life can seem meaningless, and we may struggle to find true happiness and fulfillment. It is, therefore, essential to explore the significance of meaning and purpose in a blissful life.

Purpose is the reason for which something is done or created, and it is crucial to the pursuit of happiness and fulfillment. A life without purpose is like a ship without a rudder, drifting aimlessly and without direction. Purpose provides us with a sense of direction and guides us towards our goals and aspirations. It gives our lives meaning and helps us make sense of the world around us.

Finding purpose is not always easy, and it can be a lifelong journey. However, it is a journey worth taking because living a purposeful life is one of the keys to ultimate happiness and fulfillment. In this chapter, we will explore the importance of finding purpose, the benefits of living a purposeful

12: FINDING PURPOSE: THE SIGNIFICANCE OF MEANING AND PURPOSE IN A BLISSFUL LIFE

life, and how to discover your purpose.

The Importance of Finding Purpose

Living a life of purpose is crucial to our overall well-being. It provides us with a sense of direction and gives our lives meaning. Without a sense of purpose, life can feel empty and unfulfilling. We may feel lost, unsure of what we want or where we are going.

Having a purpose can also help us to overcome obstacles and challenges. When we have a clear sense of purpose, we are more motivated and focused, and we are better able to overcome setbacks and persevere in the face of adversity.

Living a purposeful life is also essential for our mental health. Research has shown that people who have a sense of purpose are happier, more satisfied with their lives, and have a lower risk of depression and anxiety. Having a purpose gives us a reason to get up in the morning and a reason to keep going when things get tough.

The Benefits of Living a Purposeful Life

Living a purposeful life has many benefits, both for

ourselves and for those around us. Here are some of the benefits of living a purposeful life:

Greater happiness and fulfillment: When we have a clear sense of purpose, we are more likely to feel happy and fulfilled in our lives. We have a reason to get up in the morning and a sense of direction that helps us navigate the ups and downs of life.

Increased motivation and focus: When we have a purpose, we are more motivated and focused on achieving our goals. We are less likely to get sidetracked by distractions and more likely to stay on track and make progress towards our objectives.

Better mental health: Research has shown that people who have a sense of purpose are less likely to suffer from depression and anxiety. Having a purpose gives us a reason to keep going, even when things get tough, and can help us overcome obstacles and challenges.

Improved relationships: When we live a purposeful life, we are more likely to attract like-minded people who share our values and goals. This can lead to more meaningful relationships and a greater sense of community and belonging.

Greater sense of self-worth: When we have a purpose, we feel like we are contributing to something greater than ourselves. This can give us a sense of pride and self-worth, which can help us feel more confident and empowered in our lives.

How to Discover Your Purpose

Discovering your purpose is not always easy, but it is a journey worth taking. Here are some steps you can take to discover your purpose:

Identify your passions: Your passions are often a clue to your purpose. What are the things that you enjoy doing, and that bring you the most satisfaction? Make a list of your passions and consider how you could incorporate them into your life in a more meaningful way.

Consider your values: What are the values that are most important to you? Do you value honesty, integrity, kindness, or something else? Understanding your values can help you identify what is truly important to you and guide you towards a purpose that aligns with those values.

Reflect on your strengths: What are your natural talents and abilities? What do you excel at, and what comes easily to you? Your strengths can give you a clue to your purpose, as they often indicate the areas where you can make the most significant impact.

Explore your interests: What are the things that fascinate you? What topics do you find yourself researching or reading about in your free time? Your interests can also give you a clue to your purpose, as they often indicate the areas where you can make the most significant contribution.

Volunteer or try new things: Sometimes, we discover our purpose through new experiences. Volunteering or trying new things can help us explore our passions, values, strengths, and interests in a more hands-on way, which can lead us towards our purpose.

Listen to your inner voice: Finally, listen to your intuition. What does your gut tell you about what you should be doing with your life? Often, our intuition can provide valuable insights into our purpose that we might not be able to see otherwise.

Conclusion

Living a purposeful life is essential to our overall well-being and happiness. It provides us with a sense of direction, motivation, and fulfillment, and it can help us overcome obstacles and challenges. Finding purpose is a lifelong journey, but it is one that is worth taking. By identifying our passions, values, strengths, interests, and intuition, we can discover our purpose and create a life that is truly meaningful and fulfilling. Remember, the journey towards purpose is just as important as the destination, so enjoy the process and embrace the opportunities that come your way.

13: Creating a Vision: How to Set Goals and Achieve Your Dreams for a Blissful Life

Creating a Vision: How to Set Goals and Achieve Your Dreams for a Blissful Life

If you want to live a blissful life, you need to have a clear vision of what you want to achieve. Without a vision, you are like a ship without a rudder, drifting aimlessly in the sea. You need to know where you want to go and what you want to achieve in order to reach your destination.

In this chapter, we will explore the process of creating a vision for your life. We will look at how to set goals and achieve your dreams, and we will provide you with a step-by-step guide to help you get started.

Step 1: Determine Your Values

The first step in creating a vision for your life is to determine your values. Your values are the principles that guide your behavior and your decision-making. They are the things that are most important to you in life.

13: CREATING A VISION: HOW TO SET GOALS AND ACHIEVE YOUR DREAMS FOR A BLISSFUL LIFE

To determine your values, ask yourself the following questions:

– What do I stand for?

– What are my most important principles?

– What is most important to me in life?

Write down your answers to these questions. Once you have identified your values, you can use them as a guide to help you make decisions and set goals.

Step 2: Determine Your Life Purpose

The next step in creating a vision for your life is to determine your life purpose. Your life purpose is your reason for being. It is the thing that gives your life meaning and direction.

To determine your life purpose, ask yourself the following questions:

– What do I want to achieve in life?

– What is my passion?

13: CREATING A VISION: HOW TO SET GOALS AND ACHIEVE YOUR DREAMS FOR A BLISSFUL LIFE

– What is my calling?

Write down your answers to these questions. Once you have identified your life purpose, you can use it as a guide to help you set goals and make decisions.

Step 3: Set Goals

Once you have determined your values and your life purpose, the next step is to set goals. Goals are the milestones that you need to achieve in order to reach your destination.

To set goals, follow these steps:

– Write down your long-term goals. These are the things that you want to achieve in the next 5-10 years.

– Break down your long-term goals into short-term goals. These are the things that you need to achieve in the next 1-3 years.

– Break down your short-term goals into daily or weekly goals. These are the things that you need to do every day or every week in order to achieve your short-term goals.

13: CREATING A VISION: HOW TO SET GOALS AND ACHIEVE YOUR DREAMS FOR A BLISSFUL LIFE

– Write down your goals in a journal or on a vision board. This will help you visualize your goals and keep them at the forefront of your mind.

Step 4: Create an Action Plan

Once you have set your goals, the next step is to create an action plan. An action plan is a roadmap that outlines the steps that you need to take in order to achieve your goals.

To create an action plan, follow these steps:

– Identify the steps that you need to take in order to achieve your goals.

– Break down these steps into smaller, more manageable tasks.

– Assign deadlines to each task.

– Create a schedule or a to-do list to help you stay on track.

– Review your progress regularly and make adjustments as necessary.

Step 5: Stay Motivated

13: CREATING A VISION: HOW TO SET GOALS AND ACHIEVE YOUR DREAMS FOR A BLISSFUL LIFE

The final step in achieving your goals and creating a vision for your life is to stay motivated. Motivation is the fuel that drives you towards your goals.

To stay motivated, follow these tips:

– Celebrate your successes. Take time to acknowledge your accomplishments and reward yourself for a job well done.

– Stay positive. Focus on the positive aspects of your life and avoid dwelling on negative thoughts.

– Surround yourself with positive people. Seek out friends and mentors who support your vision and encourage you to reach your goals.

– Keep learning. Continuously educate yourself on the skills and knowledge you need to achieve your goals.

– Visualize your success. Use visualization techniques to imagine yourself achieving your goals and experiencing the happiness and fulfillment that comes with it.

– Practice self-care. Take care of your physical and emotional well-being by eating well, getting enough rest, and engaging in activities that make you happy and reduce stress.

By following these steps, you can create a vision for your life and achieve your goals, leading to a more blissful and fulfilling life.

However, it is important to remember that the process of achieving your goals and creating a vision for your life is not always easy. There will be setbacks, obstacles, and challenges along the way. It is important to remain persistent, resilient, and adaptable in the face of adversity.

Remember to focus on progress, not perfection, and celebrate the small successes along the way. Every step you take towards your goals is a step towards a more blissful and fulfilling life.

In conclusion, creating a vision for your life and setting goals is a crucial step in achieving ultimate happiness and fulfillment. By determining your values, identifying your life purpose, setting goals, creating an action plan, and staying motivated, you can create the life you desire and live a life filled with bliss and joy.

14: Finding Your Passion: How to Identify Your Passions and Pursue Them for Greater Fulfillment

Introduction

Bliss is something that we all strive for in life, but many of us struggle to find true happiness and fulfillment. One of the keys to achieving bliss is by finding your passion and pursuing it relentlessly. In this chapter, we will explore the importance of finding your passion, how to identify it, and how to pursue it for greater fulfillment in every aspect of your life.

The Importance of Finding Your Passion

Finding your passion is critical for achieving long-term happiness and fulfillment. When you are doing something you are passionate about, you feel energized, motivated, and fulfilled. Passion gives you a sense of purpose, and it drives you to do your best and be your best self. Without passion, life can feel mundane and unfulfilling, leaving you feeling unfulfilled and dissatisfied.

Identifying Your Passions

14: FINDING YOUR PASSION: HOW TO IDENTIFY YOUR PASSIONS AND PURSUE THEM FOR GREATER FULFILLMENT

Identifying your passions can be a challenge, especially if you've never given it much thought. Here are some steps to help you discover your passions:

Reflect on what makes you happy

Think about the things that bring you joy and happiness. What activities do you enjoy doing in your free time? What experiences have brought you the most happiness? What hobbies or interests do you have that you could spend hours doing?

Consider what you're good at

Think about your skills and talents. What do you excel at? What are some things that come easily to you? What do others often compliment you on? Your passions often align with your talents and skills.

Look for patterns

Take a look at the things that make you happy and the things you're good at. Do you see any patterns emerging? Are there common themes or areas of interest? This could give you a clue as to what your passions are.

Experiment

Try new things and explore different activities. Attend a class or workshop on something that interests you, volunteer for a cause you care about, or start a new hobby. You may discover a passion you never knew you had.

Pursuing Your Passion

Once you have identified your passion, the next step is to pursue it. Here are some tips for pursuing your passion:

Set goals

Set specific, measurable goals that will help you pursue your passion. This will give you direction and help you stay motivated.

Make time for your passion

Make time in your schedule to pursue your passion regularly. Even if it's just a few hours a week, this will help you stay committed and make progress.

14: FINDING YOUR PASSION: HOW TO IDENTIFY YOUR PASSIONS AND PURSUE THEM FOR GREATER FUL-FILLMENT

Connect with others

Connect with others who share your passion. Join a club or group, attend events, or connect with others online. This will provide you with support, encouragement, and inspiration.

Keep learning and growing

Continuously learn and grow in your area of passion. Read books, attend workshops or seminars, or take classes to deepen your knowledge and skills.

Share your passion

Share your passion with others. This can be through teaching, volunteering, or simply sharing your experiences and knowledge with others. Sharing your passion will not only help others, but it will also bring you greater fulfillment and joy.

Conclusion

Finding your passion is essential for achieving long-term

14: FINDING YOUR PASSION: HOW TO IDENTIFY YOUR PASSIONS AND PURSUE THEM FOR GREATER FUL-FILLMENT

happiness and fulfillment. By identifying your passions and pursuing them with purpose and commitment, you can unlock the secrets to ultimate bliss. Remember, passion gives you purpose and drives you to do your best and be your best self. So take the time to reflect, explore, and pursue your passions, and watch as your life transforms in ways you never thought possible.

15: Pursuing Growth and Learning: The Importance of Continuous Learning and Growth for Bliss

Bliss is a state of complete happiness and fulfillment that is sought after by many individuals. It is a state of mind that can be achieved through various means, including personal growth and continuous learning. Pursuing growth and learning is essential for attaining and maintaining a state of bliss in every aspect of your life. In this chapter, we will explore the importance of continuous learning and growth for achieving bliss and how you can incorporate these practices into your daily routine.

Why Pursuing Growth and Learning Is Important for Bliss

There are many reasons why pursuing growth and learning is crucial for achieving bliss. Here are some of the key reasons:

Personal Growth: Pursuing growth and learning helps you grow personally, allowing you to become the best version of yourself. Personal growth enables you to identify your strengths and weaknesses, work on them, and ultimately become a better person. When you are continually learning and growing, you are better equipped to handle life's challenges and to become more resilient.

Career Growth: Continuous learning and growth are also essential for career development. As the world is rapidly changing, new technologies, ideas, and trends are emerging, and it is essential to keep up with them to stay relevant and competitive in the job market. By pursuing growth and learning, you can enhance your skills, knowledge, and expertise, and become more valuable to your employer or potential employers.

Relationships: Pursuing growth and learning also has a positive impact on your relationships. When you are continually growing and learning, you become a more interesting, engaging, and inspiring person. You are better equipped to connect with others and to build more meaningful and fulfilling relationships.

Purpose: Pursuing growth and learning helps you identify your purpose in life. When you are continually learning and growing, you gain a deeper understanding of yourself and your values. You can use this knowledge to identify your

15: PURSUING GROWTH AND LEARNING: THE IMPORTANCE OF CONTINUOUS LEARNING AND GROWTH FOR BLISS

purpose in life and to pursue it with passion and conviction.

How to Incorporate Growth and Learning into Your Daily Routine

Incorporating growth and learning into your daily routine does not have to be a daunting task. Here are some tips to help you get started:

Set Goals: Setting goals is an essential step in pursuing growth and learning. Identify what you want to achieve, and set specific, measurable, and achievable goals that will help you get there. Whether it's learning a new skill, reading a book, or attending a seminar, setting goals will keep you focused and motivated.

Schedule Time: Make growth and learning a priority by scheduling time for it in your daily routine. Set aside a specific time each day or each week to focus on your personal or professional growth. This could be as simple as reading for 30 minutes each night or attending a weekly seminar.

Try New Things: Pursuing growth and learning requires stepping outside of your comfort zone and trying new things. Whether it's taking a new class, learning a new language, or traveling to a new place, trying new things can help you expand your knowledge, skills, and perspective.

Reflect and Learn from Failure: Failure is an inevitable part of the learning process. When you encounter failure, take time to reflect on what went wrong and what you can do differently next time. Use failure as an opportunity to learn and grow, rather than a setback.

Surround Yourself with Growth-Oriented People: Surrounding yourself with people who are also committed to growth and learning can provide a supportive and motivating environment. Seek out mentors, join a group or club, or attend networking events to connect with like-minded individuals.

Embrace Lifelong Learning: Pursuing growth and learning is not a one-time event, but a lifelong process. Embrace the idea of lifelong learning and commit to continuously growing and learning throughout your life.

Conclusion

15: PURSUING GROWTH AND LEARNING: THE IMPORTANCE OF CONTINUOUS LEARNING AND GROWTH FOR BLISS

Pursuing growth and learning is an essential component of achieving bliss in every aspect of your life. Personal growth, career growth, building fulfilling relationships, and identifying your purpose in life are just a few of the benefits of continuous learning and growth. By setting goals, scheduling time, trying new things, reflecting on failure, surrounding yourself with growth-oriented people, and embracing lifelong learning, you can make growth and learning a part of your daily routine. Remember, pursuing growth and learning is not a one-time event but a lifelong journey. By committing to this journey, you can unlock the secrets to ultimate happiness and fulfillment and achieve a state of bliss in every aspect of your life.

16: Embracing Change: How to Navigate Life's Changes with Grace and Ease

Change is an inevitable part of life. No matter how hard we try to hold on to what we have, change always finds a way to enter our lives. Whether it's a big change or a small one, it can disrupt our sense of stability and make us feel uneasy. However, change is not always a bad thing. In fact, it can be a great opportunity for growth and transformation. In this chapter, we will explore how to embrace change and navigate life's changes with grace and ease.

Understanding the Nature of Change

Change is a natural part of life. It can take many forms, from the small changes that happen on a daily basis, such as the weather or traffic, to the bigger changes that can completely alter the course of our lives, such as moving to a new city, starting a new job, or ending a relationship. Understanding the nature of change is the first step in embracing it. Change is neither good nor bad; it simply is. It's our reaction to change that determines whether it will be a positive or negative experience.

16: EMBRACING CHANGE: HOW TO NAVIGATE LIFE'S CHANGES WITH GRACE AND EASE

Embracing Change

Embracing change means accepting it for what it is and seeing it as an opportunity for growth and transformation. It's about letting go of our resistance to change and being open to new possibilities. It's not always easy to embrace change, especially when it's something we didn't choose or want, but it's essential if we want to live a happy and fulfilling life.

Coping with Change

Coping with change requires resilience and adaptability. It's about being able to adjust to new situations and finding ways to make the most of them. Coping with change can be challenging, but it's a skill that can be learned and developed over time. Some ways to cope with change include:

Acknowledge your feelings: Change can be difficult, and it's important to acknowledge the feelings that come with it. Allow yourself to feel sad, angry, or anxious, but also remember that these feelings will pass.

Practice self-care: Take care of yourself during times of change. Get enough sleep, eat well, exercise, and make time for activities that bring you joy.

Seek support: Reach out to friends, family, or a therapist for support during times of change. Talking about your feelings can help you process them and feel less alone.

Focus on the positive: Look for the positives in the situation and try to find opportunities for growth and learning.

Take action: Take action to make the most of the situation. Set goals and work towards them, or try new things that you've always wanted to do.

Adapting to Change

Adapting to change is about adjusting to new situations and finding ways to thrive in them. It requires a willingness to learn and grow, and a willingness to let go of old habits and ways of thinking. Adapting to change can be challenging, but it's essential if we want to live a happy and fulfilling life.

Some ways to adapt to change include:

Be open-minded: Be open to new ideas, perspectives, and ways of doing things. Embrace the unknown and be willing to take risks.

Learn new skills: Take the time to learn new skills that will help you adapt to the changes in your life. This could be anything from learning a new language to developing new work-related skills.

Find a sense of purpose: Use the change as an opportunity to find a new sense of purpose in your life. Think about what you're passionate about and how you can incorporate that into your life.

Practice mindfulness: Be present in the moment and practice mindfulness to help you cope with the stress and anxiety that can come with change.

Seeing Change as an Opportunity

Change can be scary, but it can also be an opportunity for growth and transformation. By seeing change as an opportunity, we can approach it with a positive attitude and make the most of it. Here are some ways to see change as an opportunity:

Focus on the present: Instead of dwelling on the past or

worrying about the future, focus on the present moment. This will help you stay grounded and make the most of the opportunities that come your way.

Be curious: Approach change with a sense of curiosity and wonder. Ask questions, explore new ideas, and be open to new experiences.

Take responsibility: Take responsibility for your own life and the changes that come with it. Instead of blaming others or circumstances, focus on what you can do to make the most of the situation.

Take action: Don't just wait for change to happen to you. Take action and create the change you want to see in your life.

Embrace uncertainty: Embrace the uncertainty that comes with change. Remember that uncertainty can be a good thing, as it can lead to new opportunities and experiences.

The Benefits of Embracing Change

Embracing change has many benefits, including:

16: EMBRACING CHANGE: HOW TO NAVIGATE LIFE'S CHANGES WITH GRACE AND EASE

Personal growth: Change can be a catalyst for personal growth and transformation. It can help us discover new strengths, skills, and passions.

Increased resilience: When we embrace change, we become more resilient and better able to cope with the challenges that life throws our way.

New opportunities: Change can open up new opportunities and experiences that we may not have otherwise had.

Improved relationships: Embracing change can also improve our relationships, as we become more open-minded, adaptable, and willing to see things from other people's perspectives.

Increased happiness and fulfillment: By embracing change and seeing it as an opportunity for growth and transformation, we can experience greater happiness and fulfillment in our lives.

In conclusion, change is an inevitable part of life, but it doesn't have to be a negative experience. By embracing change and seeing it as an opportunity for growth and transformation, we can navigate life's changes with grace and ease. This requires resilience, adaptability, and a willingness to let go of old habits and ways of thinking. By doing so, we can experience personal growth, new opportunities, and greater happiness and fulfillment in our lives.

17: Facing Your Fears: Overcoming Fear and Anxiety to Achieve Bliss

Introduction

Fear is an emotion that all humans experience. It is a natural response to danger or a perceived threat. While fear can be beneficial in some situations, it can also be detrimental to our happiness and fulfillment. Fear can hold us back from achieving our goals, pursuing our passions, and living the life we truly desire. Therefore, facing your fears and overcoming them is crucial for achieving ultimate happiness and fulfillment. In this chapter, we will explore the different types of fears, how they manifest in our lives, and strategies for overcoming them.

Types of Fears

There are many different types of fears, and each person may experience them differently. However, some common types of fears include:

Fear of Failure: This is the fear of not succeeding, of falling short of your own or others' expectations, and of experiencing disappointment or shame.

Fear of Rejection: This is the fear of being unloved or unaccepted, of not fitting in, and of being rejected by others.

Fear of Change: This is the fear of the unknown, of things not going as planned, and of losing control.

Fear of the Future: This is the fear of what is to come, of not knowing what will happen, and of being unprepared.

Fear of Vulnerability: This is the fear of being exposed, of showing your true self, and of being judged or criticized.

Fear of Success: This is the fear of achieving your goals, of being in the spotlight, and of having to maintain success.

Manifestations of Fear

Fears can manifest in many different ways in our lives. Some common manifestations of fear include:

Procrastination: Fear can lead to procrastination, which can prevent us from taking action towards our goals.

Self-Doubt: Fear can lead to self-doubt, which can cause us

17: FACING YOUR FEARS: OVERCOMING FEAR AND ANXIETY TO ACHIEVE BLISS

to question our abilities and limit our potential.

Avoidance: Fear can lead to avoidance, which can cause us to avoid situations that may trigger our fears.

Negative Self-Talk: Fear can lead to negative self-talk, which can create a cycle of self-doubt and self-sabotage.

Anxiety: Fear can lead to anxiety, which can cause physical symptoms such as sweating, trembling, and racing thoughts.

Strategies for Overcoming Fear

Overcoming fear is not an easy task, but it is necessary for achieving ultimate happiness and fulfillment. Here are some strategies for overcoming fear:

Identify Your Fears: The first step in overcoming fear is to identify what you are afraid of. Write down your fears and be specific.

Challenge Your Beliefs: Once you have identified your fears, challenge the beliefs that are causing them. Ask yourself if these beliefs are rational or if they are based on assumptions or past experiences.

Take Action: Taking action towards your goals is the best way to overcome fear. Start small and work your way up. Break down your goals into smaller, manageable steps and take action towards them every day.

Practice Mindfulness: Mindfulness is a powerful tool for overcoming fear. Practice being present in the moment and focus on your breath. Notice your thoughts and feelings without judgment.

Seek Support: It is important to seek support from others when facing your fears. Talk to a trusted friend or family member, or seek the help of a professional therapist or counselor.

Visualize Success: Visualize yourself succeeding in your goals and imagine how it will feel. This will help to rewire your brain and build confidence.

Celebrate Small Wins: Celebrate your small wins along the way. This will help to build momentum and keep you motivated.

17: FACING YOUR FEARS: OVERCOMING FEAR AND ANXIETY TO ACHIEVE BLISS

Conclusion

Facing your fears and overcoming them is crucial for achieving ultimate happiness and fulfillment in every aspect of your life. By identifying your fears, challenging your beliefs, taking action, practicing mindfulness, seeking support, visualizing success, and celebrating small wins, you can overcome your fears and achieve your goals.

Remember, fear is a natural part of life, but it does not have to control your life. Instead, use fear as a tool for growth and self-discovery. As you face your fears and overcome them, you will develop a sense of confidence and self-efficacy that will translate into all aspects of your life.

In addition to these strategies, it is important to cultivate a mindset of resilience and perseverance. This means accepting that setbacks and failures are a natural part of the process and using them as opportunities for growth and learning. It also means having the courage to step outside of your comfort zone and embrace new challenges and experiences.

Ultimately, the key to overcoming fear and achieving bliss is to cultivate a sense of self-awareness and self-compassion.

17: FACING YOUR FEARS: OVERCOMING FEAR AND ANXIETY TO ACHIEVE BLISS

This means being kind and gentle with yourself, recognizing your strengths and weaknesses, and accepting yourself for who you are. By cultivating these qualities, you can develop a deep sense of inner peace and contentment that will sustain you through all of life's challenges and triumphs.

So, take the time to face your fears, challenge your beliefs, and take action towards your goals. Remember to practice mindfulness, seek support, visualize success, and celebrate your small wins along the way. And most importantly, cultivate a mindset of resilience and self-compassion that will allow you to navigate life's ups and downs with grace and ease. With these tools and strategies, you can unlock the secrets to ultimate happiness and fulfillment and achieve true bliss in every aspect of your life.

18: Letting Go of Control: The Power of Surrender in Finding Happiness

Introduction:

It's easy to get caught up in the never-ending pursuit of control. We want to control our lives, our relationships, our careers, and even our emotions. But the truth is, the more we try to control everything around us, the more stressed and anxious we become. The key to finding true happiness and fulfillment lies in letting go of control and embracing the power of surrender. In this chapter, we'll explore what it means to let go of control, why it's important, and how to do it effectively.

What Does Letting Go of Control Mean?

Letting go of control means relinquishing our attachment to outcomes and accepting things as they are. It's about recognizing that there are certain things in life that we can't control, and that's okay. It's about trusting that everything will work out as it's meant to, even if it's not what we had planned or hoped for. Letting go of control doesn't mean giving up on our goals and dreams. It simply means releasing our grip on them and allowing them to unfold naturally.

Why Is Letting Go of Control Important?

Letting go of control is important for several reasons. First, it reduces stress and anxiety. When we try to control everything, we put a tremendous amount of pressure on ourselves. We worry about what might happen if things don't go according to plan. By letting go of control, we free ourselves from this constant state of worry and allow ourselves to relax and enjoy the present moment.

Second, letting go of control fosters resilience. Life is unpredictable, and things don't always go as planned. When we're able to let go of our attachment to outcomes, we're better able to bounce back from setbacks and adapt to changing circumstances.

Finally, letting go of control opens us up to new possibilities. When we're so focused on controlling every aspect of our lives, we may miss out on opportunities that come our way. By letting go of control, we allow ourselves to be more open and receptive to new experiences.

18: LETTING GO OF CONTROL: THE POWER OF SURRENDER IN FINDING HAPPINESS

How to Let Go of Control

Letting go of control is easier said than done. Here are some strategies to help you cultivate the power of surrender:

Practice Mindfulness

Mindfulness is the practice of being fully present in the moment, without judgment or attachment. When we practice mindfulness, we become more aware of our thoughts and emotions, and we're better able to observe them without getting caught up in them. This helps us to let go of control and accept things as they are.

Focus on What You Can Control

While there are many things in life that we can't control, there are also many things that we can. By focusing on what we can control, we feel more empowered and less helpless. This helps us to let go of our attachment to outcomes and focus on the process instead.

Embrace Imperfection

We're all human, and we all make mistakes. When we try to

control everything, we set ourselves up for disappointment when things inevitably go wrong. By embracing imperfection, we're able to let go of our attachment to perfection and accept things as they are.

Cultivate a Growth Mindset

A growth mindset is the belief that we can learn and grow from our experiences, even the difficult ones. When we have a growth mindset, we're better able to let go of our attachment to outcomes and focus on the process of learning and growing.

Trust the Universe

This may sound a bit woo-woo, but trusting the universe is a powerful way to let go of control. When we trust that everything is happening for a reason, even if we don't understand it at the time, we're able to surrender our attachment to outcomes and trust that everything will work out as it's meant to.

Conclusion

Letting go of control can be a difficult process, but it's an essential part of finding true happiness and fulfillment. By practicing mindfulness, focusing on what we can control, embracing imperfection, cultivating a growth mindset, and trusting the universe, we can let go of our attachment to outcomes and allow life to unfold naturally.

It's important to remember that letting go of control doesn't mean giving up on our goals and dreams. It simply means releasing our grip on them and allowing them to unfold in their own time and in their own way. When we let go of control, we create space for new possibilities and experiences to come into our lives.

In the end, finding true happiness and fulfillment is not about controlling every aspect of our lives. It's about surrendering to the present moment, accepting things as they are, and trusting that everything will work out as it's meant to. It's about embracing the power of surrender and letting go of control.

19: Cultivating Resilience: How to Bounce Back from Setbacks and Challenges

Resilience is the ability to bounce back from setbacks and challenges. It's an important trait to have because no matter how well we plan or how much effort we put in, life is full of unexpected twists and turns. Adversity can strike at any moment, and it's how we respond to it that determines whether we will emerge stronger or be consumed by it. In this chapter, we will explore the key components of resilience and provide practical tips for cultivating this trait in your life.

The Importance of Resilience

Resilience is a critical trait for achieving long-term happiness and fulfillment. Life is full of ups and downs, and those who are resilient are better able to weather the storm when things go wrong. People who lack resilience may struggle to cope with adversity and may be more likely to fall into depression or anxiety.

Resilience is also essential for personal growth. When we face challenges and setbacks, we are forced to confront our limitations and weaknesses. We can either shrink from these challenges or use them as an opportunity to learn and grow. Resilient people tend to be more open-minded and adaptable, which allows them to thrive in a constantly changing world.

Key Components of Resilience

Resilience is a complex trait that encompasses many different skills and characteristics. Here are some of the key components of resilience:

Positive Mindset: Resilient people tend to have a positive outlook on life. They see challenges as opportunities for growth and are able to find the silver lining in even the most difficult situations.

Self-Awareness: Resilience requires a deep understanding of oneself. Resilient people are aware of their strengths and weaknesses, and they are able to use this knowledge to make better decisions and cope with adversity more effectively.

Adaptability: Resilient people are able to adapt to new situations quickly. They are flexible and open-minded, which allows them to adjust their approach when things don't go according to plan.

Emotional Intelligence: Resilient people are emotionally intelligent. They are able to recognize their own emotions and the emotions of others, which allows them to navigate interpersonal relationships more effectively.

Social Support: Resilient people have a strong social support network. They have friends and family members who they can turn to for support and guidance when they face challenges.

Problem-Solving Skills: Resilient people are effective problem-solvers. They are able to identify the root cause of a problem and come up with creative solutions to overcome it.

Cultivating Resilience

Now that we've discussed the importance of resilience and the key components that make up this trait, let's explore some practical tips for cultivating resilience in your life.

19: CULTIVATING RESILIENCE: HOW TO BOUNCE BACK FROM SETBACKS AND CHALLENGES

Practice Self-Care: Self-care is essential for building resilience. This means taking care of your physical, emotional, and spiritual needs. Make sure you're getting enough sleep, eating a healthy diet, and engaging in regular exercise. Take time to do things that bring you joy, whether it's reading a book, going for a walk, or spending time with friends.

Build a Support Network: Having a strong support network is critical for resilience. Surround yourself with people who are positive, supportive, and caring. Reach out to friends and family members when you need help or guidance. Join a support group or online community that focuses on resilience and personal growth.

Cultivate a Growth Mindset: A growth mindset is the belief that you can learn and grow from challenges and setbacks. Embrace challenges as opportunities for growth and learning. Instead of giving up when things get difficult, focus on what you can learn from the experience and how you can use that knowledge to become stronger.

Practice Mindfulness: Mindfulness is the practice of being present in the moment and observing your thoughts and emotions without judgment. Mindfulness can help you build emotional resilience by allowing you to become more aware of your thoughts and emotions, and developing a greater ability to regulate them. You can practice mindfulness through meditation, yoga, or simply taking a few minutes each day to focus on your breath.

Develop Problem-Solving Skills: Developing problem-solving skills can help you become more resilient by allowing you to identify the root cause of a problem and come up with effective solutions. One effective problem-solving technique is to break down a problem into smaller, more manageable steps. This can help you approach the problem in a more systematic and logical way, and increase your chances of finding a solution.

Embrace Failure: Failure is a natural part of life, and it's impossible to avoid it entirely. Resilient people embrace failure as a learning opportunity and use it to fuel personal growth. Instead of dwelling on their mistakes, they use them as a springboard to become better and more resilient.

Focus on Gratitude: Gratitude is a powerful tool for building resilience. By focusing on what you're grateful for, you can cultivate a more positive outlook on life and increase your resilience in the face of challenges. Take time each day to reflect on what you're grateful for, whether it's a supportive friend or family member, a beautiful sunset, or a delicious meal.

Set Realistic Goals: Setting realistic goals can help you build resilience by giving you a sense of purpose and direction. When you set realistic goals, you're more likely to achieve them, which can boost your confidence and sense of self-efficacy. Make sure your goals are challenging enough to push you outside of your comfort zone, but not so difficult that they feel impossible to achieve.

Practice Self-Compassion: Self-compassion is the practice of treating yourself with kindness and understanding, especially during difficult times. Instead of criticizing yourself for your mistakes or shortcomings, practice self-compassion by speaking to yourself in a kind and supportive manner. This can help you build resilience by giving you the emotional resources you need to face challenges with courage and determination.

Seek Professional Help: Finally, if you're struggling to build resilience on your own, don't hesitate to seek professional help. A therapist or counselor can provide you with the tools and support you need to overcome challenges and become more resilient. They can also help you identify any underlying mental health issues that may be affecting your ability to build resilience.

In conclusion, resilience is a critical trait for achieving long-term happiness and fulfillment. By cultivating resilience, you can bounce back from setbacks and challenges, and become more adaptable, emotionally intelligent, and effective problem-solvers. Use the tips outlined in this chapter to start building resilience in your own life today, and watch as your ability to thrive in the face of adversity grows stronger with each passing day.

20: Building Strong Relationships: The Importance of Connection and Community for Bliss

Relationships are an essential part of the human experience. From the moment we are born, we begin to form connections with the people around us. As we grow older, these connections become more complex, and we seek out deeper relationships with others. Building strong relationships is a key component of achieving happiness and fulfillment in life. In this chapter, we will explore the importance of connection and community for achieving bliss, as well as strategies for building and maintaining strong relationships.

The Importance of Connection

Humans are social creatures by nature. We crave connection and interaction with others. Research has shown that social support is crucial for mental health and well-being. Studies have shown that people who have strong relationships with friends and family are less likely to experience depression, anxiety, and other mental health issues.

Connection also plays an important role in physical health.

20: BUILDING STRONG RELATIONSHIPS: THE IMPORTANCE OF CONNECTION AND COMMUNITY FOR BLISS

Studies have found that social isolation can have negative effects on the body, including increased inflammation, high blood pressure, and a weakened immune system. On the other hand, people who have strong social support are more likely to recover from illness and live longer, healthier lives.

Connection and community are also essential for personal growth and development. When we interact with others, we learn from their experiences and perspectives. We can gain new insights and ideas, and develop a deeper understanding of ourselves and the world around us. Through connection and community, we can also find support and encouragement as we pursue our goals and aspirations.

Building Strong Relationships

Building strong relationships takes time and effort. It requires a willingness to be vulnerable, to communicate openly and honestly, and to put in the work necessary to maintain the relationship. Here are some strategies for building and maintaining strong relationships:

Practice Active Listening

20: BUILDING STRONG RELATIONSHIPS: THE IMPORTANCE OF CONNECTION AND COMMUNITY FOR BLISS

One of the most important skills in building strong relationships is active listening. This means giving your full attention to the person speaking, and taking the time to understand their perspective. It also involves asking questions and clarifying your understanding, so that you can ensure you are on the same page.

Be Authentic

Authenticity is key to building strong relationships. This means being true to yourself, and sharing your thoughts and feelings honestly. When we are authentic, we create a sense of trust and safety in our relationships, which can lead to deeper connections.

Show Empathy

Empathy is the ability to understand and share the feelings of another person. When we show empathy, we demonstrate that we care about the other person and their experiences. This can help to strengthen the bond between us and create a deeper sense of connection.

Practice Forgiveness

20: BUILDING STRONG RELATIONSHIPS: THE IM-PORTANCE OF CONNECTION AND COMMUNITY FOR BLISS

No relationship is perfect, and conflicts are bound to arise. Practicing forgiveness is essential for maintaining strong relationships. This means letting go of grudges and resentments, and working to repair the relationship when things go wrong.

Make Time for Connection

Building strong relationships requires time and effort. It's important to prioritize connection in your life, and make time for the people who are important to you. Whether it's scheduling regular date nights with your partner, or setting aside time for a weekly phone call with a friend, making time for connection can help to strengthen your relationships.

Cultivate Shared Experiences

Shared experiences are a powerful way to build connections with others. Whether it's traveling together, trying a new hobby, or simply spending time together, shared experiences can create memories and bonds that last a lifetime.

Creating a Purposeful Life through Connection and Community

Connection and community are essential components of a purposeful life. When we connect with others, we can find support and encouragement as we pursue our goals and aspirations. We can also find meaning and purpose through our connections with others, as we work together to create positive change in the world.

Here are some ways to cultivate connection and community in your life:

Volunteer

Volunteering is a powerful way to connect with others and create a sense of community. When we volunteer, we are working together with others towards a common goal, and we are able to see the positive impact that we can have on the world around us. Whether it's volunteering at a local shelter, participating in a community garden project, or joining a service club, volunteering can help to strengthen our sense of connection and purpose.

Join a Group or Club

20: BUILDING STRONG RELATIONSHIPS: THE IMPORTANCE OF CONNECTION AND COMMUNITY FOR BLISS

Joining a group or club is another way to connect with like-minded individuals and build a sense of community. Whether it's a book club, a hiking group, or a sports team, participating in a group activity can help to create a sense of belonging and camaraderie.

Attend Events and Gatherings

Attending events and gatherings is a great way to connect with others and experience new things. Whether it's a concert, a festival, or a community event, attending these types of gatherings can help to build connections and create a sense of community.

Connect Online

In today's digital age, connecting with others online is easier than ever before. Whether it's through social media, online forums, or other online communities, connecting with others online can help to build connections and create a sense of community.

Practice Gratitude

20: BUILDING STRONG RELATIONSHIPS: THE IM-PORTANCE OF CONNECTION AND COMMUNITY FOR BLISS

Gratitude is an important component of building strong relationships and creating a purposeful life. When we express gratitude for the people and experiences in our lives, we are able to cultivate a sense of connection and appreciation for the world around us. This can help to strengthen our relationships and create a more fulfilling life.

In Conclusion

Building strong relationships is an essential component of achieving happiness and fulfillment in life. Connection and community are important for mental and physical health, personal growth and development, and creating a purposeful life. By practicing active listening, authenticity, empathy, forgiveness, and making time for connection, we can build strong relationships with those around us. Additionally, by volunteering, joining groups or clubs, attending events and gatherings, connecting online, and practicing gratitude, we can cultivate a sense of community and purpose in our lives. Ultimately, building strong relationships and creating a sense of connection and community is a key component of achieving bliss in every aspect of our lives.

21: Communicating Effectively: How to Communicate Your Needs and Desires for Better Relationships

Introduction

Effective communication is the foundation of healthy relationships. Whether you're communicating with your partner, family, friends, or colleagues, being able to express your needs and desires in a clear and respectful manner is crucial to building strong connections and avoiding misunderstandings. In this chapter, we'll explore the key elements of effective communication and provide you with practical tips to help you communicate your needs and desires for better relationships.

Understanding Communication

Communication is the process of transmitting information from one person to another. It involves both verbal and nonverbal cues, such as tone of voice, facial expressions, and body language. Effective communication is characterized by a mutual understanding between the parties involved.

There are several key elements of effective communication:

Clarity: Communicate clearly and concisely, using simple language and avoiding jargon or technical terms that the other person may not understand.

Active Listening: Listen actively, paying attention to both verbal and nonverbal cues, and demonstrating that you are fully engaged in the conversation.

Empathy: Put yourself in the other person's shoes, and try to understand their perspective and feelings.

Respect: Show respect for the other person's opinions and ideas, even if you disagree with them.

Timing: Choose the right time and place to have the conversation, when both parties are calm and focused.

Nonverbal Communication: Be aware of your nonverbal cues, such as tone of voice, facial expressions, and body language, and make sure they align with your verbal message.

21: COMMUNICATING EFFECTIVELY: HOW TO COM-MUNICATE YOUR NEEDS AND DESIRES FOR BETTER RELATIONSHIPS

Feedback: Provide feedback to the other person to ensure that they understand your message, and encourage them to provide feedback to you.

Clarification: Clarify any misunderstandings or confusion immediately, to avoid any negative impact on the relationship.

Tips for Effective Communication

Be clear and concise: When communicating your needs and desires, be clear and concise. Use simple language and avoid using jargon or technical terms that the other person may not understand.

Listen actively: Listen actively to the other person, paying attention to both verbal and nonverbal cues. Demonstrate that you are fully engaged in the conversation by maintaining eye contact and nodding your head.

Show empathy: Try to understand the other person's perspective and feelings. Put yourself in their shoes, and try to see things from their point of view.

21: COMMUNICATING EFFECTIVELY: HOW TO COMMUNICATE YOUR NEEDS AND DESIRES FOR BETTER RELATIONSHIPS

Avoid criticism: Avoid criticizing the other person or their actions, as this can put them on the defensive and make it difficult to have a productive conversation.

Use "I" statements: Use "I" statements to communicate your needs and desires. For example, say "I feel hurt when you ignore me" instead of "You always ignore me."

Be specific: Be specific when communicating your needs and desires. For example, say "I would like to spend more quality time together" instead of "We should spend more time together."

Choose the right time and place: Choose the right time and place to have the conversation, when both parties are calm and focused. Avoid having the conversation when either of you is upset or distracted.

Use nonverbal communication: Be aware of your nonverbal cues, such as tone of voice, facial expressions, and body language, and make sure they align with your verbal message.

Provide feedback: Provide feedback to the other person to ensure that they understand your message. Encourage them to provide feedback to you as well.

Clarify misunderstandings: Clarify any misunderstandings or confusion immediately, to avoid any negative impact on the relationship.

Conclusion

Effective communication is the foundation of healthy relationships. By understanding the key elements of effective communication and following these practical tips, you can communicate your needs and desires in a clear and respectful manner, and build stronger connections with the people in your life. Remember to listen actively, show empathy, and use "I" statements to express your feelings and desires. Be specific and choose the right time and place for the conversation. Use nonverbal communication to reinforce your message and provide feedback to ensure that you are understood. And if there are any misunderstandings, clarify them immediately to avoid any negative impact on the relationship.

Communication is not always easy, and it takes practice to

become an effective communicator. But by investing time
and effort into improving your communication skills, you
can unlock the secrets to ultimate happiness and fulfillment
in every aspect of your life. Whether it's your romantic relationships, your friendships, or your professional connections, effective communication is the key to building strong,
meaningful relationships that will last a lifetime.

So, take some time to reflect on your communication skills
and identify areas where you could improve. Practice active
listening, use "I" statements, and be specific and clear when
communicating your needs and desires. With time and effort, you'll find that your relationships become stronger and
more fulfilling, and you'll experience a greater sense of happiness and contentment in every aspect of your life.

22: Practicing Empathy and Compassion: The Role of Kindness and Empathy in Building Strong Relationships

Empathy and compassion are two powerful tools for building strong relationships and living a fulfilling life. Empathy is the ability to understand and share the feelings of another person, while compassion is the feeling of wanting to help someone who is suffering. When we practice empathy and compassion, we create a positive environment around us and improve our own well-being.

In this chapter, we will explore the importance of empathy and compassion, how to develop these traits, and how to apply them in our daily lives to build stronger relationships and experience greater happiness and fulfillment.

Why Empathy and Compassion Are Important

Empathy and compassion are critical for building strong relationships because they enable us to understand and connect with others on a deeper level. When we practice empathy, we can put ourselves in someone else's shoes and understand their perspective, even if we don't agree with it. This helps us communicate more effectively and avoid misunderstandings.

Compassion, on the other hand, allows us to be there for others when they need us. It's the feeling of wanting to help someone who is suffering, even if we don't know them very well. When we show compassion, we create a sense of belonging and community, which can help us feel more connected and fulfilled.

Research has shown that practicing empathy and compassion can have numerous benefits for our mental and physical health. For example, a study published in the Journal of Social Psychology found that practicing empathy can reduce stress and improve our overall well-being. Similarly, a study published in the Journal of Happiness Studies found that practicing compassion can increase our happiness and life satisfaction.

How to Develop Empathy and Compassion

Fortunately, empathy and compassion are not fixed traits -

they can be developed and improved over time. Here are some strategies for developing these important traits:

Practice active listening: One of the most important components of empathy is active listening. When we actively listen to someone, we give them our full attention and show that we care about what they have to say. This can help us understand their perspective and build stronger relationships.

Put yourself in someone else's shoes: When trying to understand someone else's perspective, it can be helpful to imagine yourself in their situation. This can help you see things from their point of view and better understand their feelings and experiences.

Practice self-compassion: It's difficult to show compassion to others if we don't first practice self-compassion. This means being kind to ourselves and treating ourselves with the same understanding and care that we would offer to a friend.

Practice gratitude: Practicing gratitude can help us appreciate the good things in our lives and feel more connected to others. When we focus on the positive, it can be easier to feel empathy and compassion for others.

Practice mindfulness: Mindfulness can help us become more aware of our thoughts and feelings, which can help us better understand ourselves and others. When we are mindful, we can also be more present and attentive in our relationships, which can strengthen our connections with others.

Applying Empathy and Compassion in Daily Life

Once we have developed our empathy and compassion skills, it's important to apply them in our daily lives. Here are some ways to do so:

Practice random acts of kindness: Doing something kind for someone else, even if it's just holding the door open or offering a compliment, can make a big difference in someone's day. These small acts of kindness can also help us feel more connected to others and increase our own happiness.

22: PRACTICING EMPATHY AND COMPASSION: THE ROLE OF KINDNESS AND EMPATHY IN BUILDING STRONG RELATIONSHIPS

Be present in conversations: When we're having a conversation with someone, it's important to be fully present and give them our full attention. This means avoiding distractions like our phone or other devices, and actively listening to what they're saying. By doing so, we show that we value their perspective and care about what they have to say.

Practice empathy in conflicts: When conflicts arise, it can be difficult to understand the other person's perspective. However, by practicing empathy, we can better understand their point of view and work towards a resolution that benefits both parties. This can help prevent further conflict and strengthen our relationships.

Show compassion to those in need: Whether it's a friend going through a tough time or a stranger on the street, showing compassion to those in need can make a big difference in their lives. This can be as simple as offering a kind word or a listening ear, or as involved as volunteering or donating to a charity.

Practice forgiveness: Forgiveness can be a difficult thing to do, but it's an important aspect of empathy and compassion. When we forgive others for their mistakes, we show that we understand their humanity and are willing to move past their actions. This can help repair damaged relationships and bring us closer together.

Conclusion

Empathy and compassion are critical components of building strong relationships and living a fulfilling life. By developing these traits and applying them in our daily lives, we can create a positive environment around us and improve our own well-being. Whether it's practicing active listening, showing compassion to those in need, or practicing forgiveness, there are many ways to incorporate empathy and compassion into our daily lives. By doing so, we can unlock the secrets to ultimate happiness and fulfillment.

23: Forgiveness and Letting Go: How Forgiveness Can Bring Healing and Joy

Forgiveness is a powerful tool that can bring healing and joy into our lives. It is the act of letting go of the anger and resentment we hold towards someone who has wronged us, and choosing to move on from the hurt. Forgiveness is not easy, but it is necessary if we want to experience true happiness and fulfillment.

In this chapter, we will explore the concept of forgiveness and its benefits. We will also discuss some practical tips on how to forgive and let go, so that you can experience the joy and peace that comes with it.

The Importance of Forgiveness

Forgiveness is important for several reasons. First, holding on to anger and resentment can be damaging to our mental and emotional health. When we hold on to negative emotions, we are more likely to experience stress, anxiety, and depression. This can lead to physical health problems as well, such as high blood pressure and heart disease.

Forgiveness also helps us to heal from the hurt caused by the person who wronged us. When we choose to forgive, we release ourselves from the pain and suffering that comes with holding a grudge. It allows us to move on from the past and focus on the present and future.

Finally, forgiveness is essential for building and maintaining healthy relationships. When we hold on to anger and resentment, it can create a barrier between us and the person we are angry with. Forgiveness allows us to break down that barrier and open the door to communication and understanding.

The Benefits of Forgiveness

Forgiveness has numerous benefits for our mental, emotional, and physical health. Here are just a few of the ways that forgiveness can improve our lives:

Reduced Stress and Anxiety: When we forgive, we let go of the negative emotions that can cause stress and anxiety. This can lead to improved mental and emotional health, as well as better physical health.

23: FORGIVENESS AND LETTING GO: HOW FORGIVE-NESS CAN BRING HEALING AND JOY

Improved Relationships: Forgiveness can help to repair damaged relationships and build stronger ones. When we forgive, we are more likely to communicate openly and honestly with the person who wronged us, which can lead to greater understanding and empathy.

Greater Self-Awareness: Forgiveness can help us to become more self-aware and introspective. When we forgive, we are forced to confront our own negative emotions and work through them. This can lead to greater self-awareness and personal growth.

Increased Happiness: Forgiveness can lead to greater happiness and fulfillment in our lives. When we let go of negative emotions, we are free to focus on the positive aspects of our lives and experience greater joy and contentment.

How to Forgive and Let Go

Forgiveness is not always easy, but it is possible. Here are some practical tips for forgiving and letting go:

Acknowledge Your Emotions: Before you can forgive, you need to acknowledge your own emotions. This means accepting that you are angry, hurt, or resentful, and allowing yourself to feel those emotions fully.

Practice Empathy: Try to see the situation from the other person's perspective. This can help you to understand why they did what they did, and can make it easier to forgive them.

Communicate Your Feelings: Talk to the person who wronged you and express how their actions made you feel. This can help to clear the air and open the door to forgiveness.

Make a Conscious Choice to Forgive: Forgiveness is a choice. You need to make a conscious decision to let go of the anger and resentment you hold towards the other person.

Focus on the Present: Letting go of the past can be difficult, but it is essential if you want to move on. Focus on the present moment and what you can do to create a positive future.

Practice Self-Care: Forgiveness can be a difficult process,

and it's important to take care of yourself during this time. Make sure to prioritize self-care activities, such as exercise, meditation, or spending time with loved ones.

Seek Professional Help: If you're struggling to forgive and let go on your own, it may be helpful to seek professional help. A therapist or counselor can provide guidance and support as you work through the forgiveness process.

The Power of Forgiveness

Forgiveness is a powerful tool that can bring healing and joy into our lives. It allows us to let go of the anger and resentment that can hold us back from experiencing true happiness and fulfillment. By practicing forgiveness, we can improve our mental, emotional, and physical health, build and maintain healthy relationships, and experience greater happiness and contentment in our lives.

Remember, forgiveness is not always easy, but it is possible. By acknowledging your emotions, practicing empathy, communicating your feelings, making a conscious choice to forgive, focusing on the present, practicing self-care, and seeking professional help if needed, you can experience the power of forgiveness and let go of the hurt that is holding you back.

24: The Power of Authenticity: How to Be True to Yourself and Build Authentic Relationships

Introduction:

Authenticity is the key to living a fulfilling and satisfying life. It means being true to yourself, embracing your strengths and weaknesses, and being honest with those around you. Authenticity is a powerful tool for building meaningful relationships, creating a purposeful life, and achieving ultimate happiness and fulfillment. In this chapter, we will explore the power of authenticity and how you can be true to yourself and build authentic relationships.

What is Authenticity?

Authenticity is the quality of being genuine, honest, and true to oneself. It means being able to express your thoughts, feelings, and beliefs without fear of judgment or rejection. Authenticity is about accepting and embracing your unique self and not conforming to societal norms or expectations. When you are authentic, you are true to yourself and to others.

24: THE POWER OF AUTHENTICITY: HOW TO BE TRUE TO YOURSELF AND BUILD AUTHENTIC RELATIONSHIPS

The Importance of Authenticity:

Authenticity is essential for living a fulfilling and satisfying life. When you are authentic, you are able to create meaningful relationships based on honesty and trust. You are able to express your thoughts, feelings, and beliefs without fear of judgment or rejection. Authenticity also enables you to make decisions based on your values and beliefs, rather than conforming to societal norms or expectations.

Authenticity is also important for your mental health and well-being. When you are true to yourself, you are able to accept and embrace your strengths and weaknesses. You are able to develop a positive self-image and improve your self-esteem. Authenticity also allows you to develop a sense of purpose and meaning in your life, which can lead to greater happiness and fulfillment.

How to Be True to Yourself:

Being true to yourself requires self-awareness, self-acceptance, and self-expression. Here are some steps you can take to be true to yourself:

24: THE POWER OF AUTHENTICITY: HOW TO BE TRUE TO YOURSELF AND BUILD AUTHENTIC RELATIONSHIPS

Know your values and beliefs: To be true to yourself, you need to know what you stand for. Take some time to identify your values and beliefs. Ask yourself what is important to you and what you believe in.

Accept your strengths and weaknesses: Nobody is perfect, and we all have strengths and weaknesses. Accepting your strengths and weaknesses is an essential part of being true to yourself. Embrace your strengths and work on improving your weaknesses.

Express your thoughts and feelings: Expressing your thoughts and feelings is a powerful way to be true to yourself. Speak up when you disagree with something or when you have something important to say. Don't be afraid to show your emotions.

Set boundaries: Setting boundaries is an important part of being true to yourself. It means saying no when you need to and setting limits on what you are willing to tolerate. When you set boundaries, you are showing respect for yourself and your needs.

24: THE POWER OF AUTHENTICITY: HOW TO BE TRUE TO YOURSELF AND BUILD AUTHENTIC RELATION-SHIPS

How to Build Authentic Relationships:

Building authentic relationships requires honesty, trust, and vulnerability. Here are some steps you can take to build authentic relationships:

Be honest: Honesty is the foundation of authentic relationships. Be honest about your thoughts, feelings, and intentions. Don't hide your true self or pretend to be someone you're not.

Listen actively: Listening is an important part of building authentic relationships. When you listen actively, you show that you care and that you are interested in what the other person has to say.

Be vulnerable: Being vulnerable means sharing your thoughts, feelings, and experiences in a way that is honest and authentic. When you are vulnerable, you allow others to see the real you and to connect with you on a deeper level.

Show empathy: Empathy is the ability to understand and share the feelings of others. When you show empathy, you are able to connect with others on an emotional level and build authentic relationships based on trust and understanding.

Conclusion:

Authenticity is a powerful tool for building meaningful relationships, creating a purposeful life, and achieving ultimate happiness and fulfillment. By being true to yourself and building authentic relationships, you can live a life that is truly fulfilling and satisfying.

Remember, being authentic doesn't mean being perfect. It means embracing your unique self and being honest with yourself and others. It means accepting and embracing your strengths and weaknesses, setting boundaries, expressing your thoughts and feelings, and being true to your values and beliefs.

Building authentic relationships requires honesty, trust, and vulnerability. By being honest, listening actively, being vulnerable, and showing empathy, you can build relationships that are based on trust and understanding.

In today's world, it can be challenging to be authentic and

24: THE POWER OF AUTHENTICITY: HOW TO BE TRUE TO YOURSELF AND BUILD AUTHENTIC RELATION-SHIPS

build authentic relationships. Social media, societal expectations, and the pressure to conform can make it difficult to be true to yourself. However, by taking the steps outlined in this chapter, you can live a life that is true to yourself and build authentic relationships that bring joy and fulfillment to your life.

In conclusion, authenticity is a powerful tool for living a fulfilling and satisfying life. By being true to yourself and building authentic relationships, you can achieve ultimate happiness and fulfillment in every aspect of your life. So embrace your unique self, be honest, and build relationships based on trust and understanding. The power of authenticity is truly life-changing, and it is within your reach.

25: Cultivating Gratitude in Relationships: The Importance of Appreciation and Gratitude in Building Strong Connections

Relationships are the backbone of our lives. Whether it's our family, friends, or significant others, the people we surround ourselves with can greatly impact our happiness and sense of fulfillment. And while there are many different factors that contribute to a strong and healthy relationship, one of the most important is the practice of gratitude.

Gratitude is a powerful emotion that can have a profound impact on our lives. When we feel grateful, we focus on the positive aspects of our lives and feel a sense of appreciation for the people and things around us. This positive mindset can help us cultivate more positive emotions, like joy and contentment, which in turn can lead to greater overall happiness and well-being.

In the context of relationships, gratitude can play a particularly important role. When we express gratitude towards our loved ones, we show them that we appreciate them and value their presence in our lives. This can help to build a

25: CULTIVATING GRATITUDE IN RELATIONSHIPS: THE IMPORTANCE OF APPRECIATION AND GRATITUDE IN BUILDING STRONG CONNECTIONS

stronger connection between us and our partner, friends, or family members, and can help to foster a more positive and supportive relationship overall.

So, how can we cultivate gratitude in our relationships? One of the most important things is to make a conscious effort to focus on the positive aspects of our relationships, rather than the negative. It can be easy to get caught up in the day-to-day challenges and conflicts that arise in any relationship, but by making an effort to look for the good things, we can shift our focus to what's truly important.

One way to do this is to start a gratitude journal specifically focused on your relationships. Take some time each day to reflect on the positive aspects of your relationship with your partner, friends, or family members, and write down your thoughts in your journal. This can help to reinforce positive emotions and increase feelings of appreciation and gratitude.

Another important way to cultivate gratitude in relationships is to express it to our loved ones directly. This can be as simple as saying "thank you" when they do something kind or thoughtful, or taking the time to write a heartfelt note or card expressing our gratitude and appreciation for their presence in our lives.

When we express gratitude to our loved ones, we not only show them that we appreciate them, but we also reinforce our own positive emotions and deepen our connection with them. By making gratitude a regular part of our relationships, we can help to create a more positive and supportive environment that can help us all to thrive and grow together.

Of course, gratitude is not always easy, especially in the face of difficult or challenging situations. But even in these moments, cultivating a sense of gratitude can help to shift our perspective and focus on the positive aspects of our relationships.

For example, if we're going through a difficult time with our partner, rather than focusing on the negatives, we can try to focus on the positive aspects of our relationship, such as the love and support we've received in the past, or the positive traits and qualities that drew us to our partner in the first place. By focusing on these positives, we can help to shift our mindset and create a more positive and supportive environment for our relationship to thrive.

In conclusion, cultivating gratitude in relationships is an important part of building strong and healthy connections with our loved ones. By focusing on the positive aspects of our relationships and expressing gratitude and appreciation for our partners, friends, and family members, we can help to deepen our connections, reinforce positive emotions, and create a more positive and supportive environment for us all to thrive and grow together.

26: Living with Intention: How to Live a Purposeful and Intentional Life for Greater Bliss

Have you ever felt like you're simply going through the motions of life without any real direction or purpose? Do you feel like you're stuck in a rut and that your life lacks meaning? If so, you're not alone. Many people struggle to find their purpose in life, and as a result, they feel unfulfilled and unhappy.

However, the good news is that you don't have to settle for a life without purpose or meaning. By living with intention, you can create a purposeful and intentional life that brings you joy, fulfillment, and a sense of direction. In this chapter, we will explore what it means to live with intention, how to identify your values and goals, and practical steps you can take to live a more purposeful and intentional life.

What Does It Mean to Live with Intention?

Living with intention means being purposeful and deliberate in the way you approach your life. It means being mindful of your thoughts, actions, and behaviors and making choices that align with your values and goals. Living with

26: LIVING WITH INTENTION: HOW TO LIVE A PURPOSEFUL AND INTENTIONAL LIFE FOR GREATER BLISS

intention requires you to be proactive in shaping your life, rather than simply reacting to what life throws your way.

Living with intention involves being present and fully engaged in each moment, rather than mindlessly going through the motions. It means taking the time to reflect on your experiences, learn from them, and use that knowledge to make intentional choices that move you closer to your goals.

Identifying Your Values and Goals

To live with intention, you need to have a clear understanding of your values and goals. Your values are the principles and beliefs that guide your behavior and decision-making. Your goals are the specific outcomes you want to achieve in your life.

To identify your values, start by reflecting on what is most important to you. Ask yourself questions like:

– What do I stand for?

– What principles do I believe in?

26: LIVING WITH INTENTION: HOW TO LIVE A PURPOSEFUL AND INTENTIONAL LIFE FOR GREATER BLISS

– What qualities do I admire in others?

– What brings me the most joy and fulfillment in life?

As you answer these questions, you'll begin to identify the core values that guide your life. Some common values include honesty, compassion, integrity, growth, and connection.

Once you have a clear understanding of your values, you can start setting goals that align with them. Your goals should be specific, measurable, achievable, relevant, and time-bound (SMART). For example, if one of your values is growth, you might set a goal to learn a new skill or take a class in an area that interests you.

Living with Intention: Practical Steps

Now that you have identified your values and goals, it's time to start living with intention. Here are some practical steps you can take to live a more purposeful and intentional life:

Set daily intentions. Each morning, take a few moments to set an intention for the day. Your intention could be something as simple as "I intend to be present and engaged in each moment" or "I intend to prioritize self-care today."

Practice mindfulness. Mindfulness is the practice of being present and fully engaged in each moment. When you're mindful, you're able to observe your thoughts and feelings without judgment. This can help you make more intentional choices and respond to situations in a way that aligns with your values and goals.

Create a vision board. A vision board is a visual representation of your goals and aspirations. It can help you stay focused on what's important to you and motivate you to take intentional action towards achieving your goals.

Prioritize self-care. Taking care of yourself is an essential component of living with intention. Make sure you're getting enough sleep, eating a healthy diet, and engaging in activities that bring you joy and fulfillment.

Practice gratitude. Taking the time to acknowledge and appreciate the good things in your life can help you cultivate a positive mindset and increase your overall sense of happiness and fulfillment. Make a habit of writing down three things you're grateful for each day.

Set boundaries. Setting boundaries is an important part of living with intention. It means being clear about your limits and communicating them to others. This can help you avoid overcommitting yourself and ensure that you're making choices that align with your values and goals.

Be intentional with your time. Time is a finite resource, so it's important to use it wisely. Make a conscious effort to prioritize the activities and relationships that are most important to you, and avoid wasting time on things that don't align with your values and goals.

Take intentional action towards your goals. Setting goals is only the first step - you also need to take intentional action towards achieving them. Break your goals down into smaller, actionable steps, and make a plan to accomplish them.

Reflect regularly. Reflection is a powerful tool for living with intention. Set aside time each week to reflect on your experiences, identify what's working and what's not, and make

26: LIVING WITH INTENTION: HOW TO LIVE A PURPOSEFUL AND INTENTIONAL LIFE FOR GREATER BLISS

adjustments as needed.

Living with intention is a lifelong journey, and it's normal to experience setbacks and challenges along the way. However, by staying committed to your values and goals and making intentional choices, you can create a purposeful and intentional life that brings you joy and fulfillment.

Conclusion

Living with intention is about taking control of your life and making choices that align with your values and goals. By being mindful, setting daily intentions, practicing self-care, and taking intentional action towards your goals, you can create a purposeful and intentional life that brings you happiness and fulfillment. Remember, living with intention is a journey, not a destination, so be patient with yourself and stay committed to your values and goals.

27: Embracing Your Unique Gifts: How to Tap into Your Unique Talents and Strengths for Fulfillment

As human beings, we are all blessed with unique talents and strengths that make us who we are. These gifts are an integral part of our identity, and they play a critical role in our pursuit of happiness and fulfillment. Unfortunately, many people never fully tap into their unique gifts, and as a result, they go through life feeling unfulfilled and dissatisfied.

In this chapter, we will explore the importance of embracing your unique gifts and how to tap into your talents and strengths to achieve fulfillment in every aspect of your life.

Understanding Your Unique Gifts

Before you can tap into your unique gifts, it's important to understand what they are. Your unique gifts are the skills, talents, and strengths that come naturally to you. They are the things that you excel at and the activities that bring you joy and fulfillment. Your unique gifts are not just the things that you are good at; they are the things that make you stand out from others.

27: EMBRACING YOUR UNIQUE GIFTS: HOW TO TAP INTO YOUR UNIQUE TALENTS AND STRENGTHS FOR FULFILLMENT

Your unique gifts can be anything from creative talents like writing or painting to more practical skills like problem-solving or leadership. They can be physical abilities like athleticism or coordination or intellectual strengths like critical thinking or analytical skills. Whatever your unique gifts are, they are an essential part of who you are, and embracing them is key to achieving ultimate happiness and fulfillment.

Embracing Your Unique Gifts

Once you understand your unique gifts, the next step is to embrace them fully. Embracing your unique gifts means acknowledging and accepting them as a fundamental part of who you are. It means allowing yourself to be proud of your talents and strengths and using them to your advantage.

To embrace your unique gifts, start by taking an inventory of your strengths and weaknesses. Focus on the things that come naturally to you and the activities that bring you joy and fulfillment. Once you have a clear understanding of your unique gifts, make a conscious effort to incorporate them into your daily life. This could mean pursuing a career that aligns with your strengths, volunteering your time in areas that showcase your talents, or simply spending more time doing activities that bring you joy.

Tapping into Your Unique Gifts

Tapping into your unique gifts requires more than just embracing them. It also requires a willingness to explore new opportunities and take risks. You may need to step out of your comfort zone and try new things to fully tap into your talents and strengths.

One way to tap into your unique gifts is to seek out opportunities that challenge you to use them. For example, if you have a talent for writing, consider starting a blog or submitting articles to publications. If you have a gift for public speaking, seek out opportunities to give presentations or speeches. The more you use your unique gifts, the stronger they will become.

Another way to tap into your unique gifts is to seek out mentorship and guidance from others who share your talents and strengths. Surrounding yourself with like-minded individuals can be a powerful way to learn and grow, and it can also help you develop a sense of community around your gifts.

Cultivating Fulfillment Through Your Unique Gifts

Embracing and tapping into your unique gifts can be a powerful way to cultivate fulfillment in your life. When you use your talents and strengths, you feel a sense of purpose and accomplishment that can be difficult to achieve in other areas of your life. Your unique gifts can also help you connect with others and create meaningful relationships.

To cultivate fulfillment through your unique gifts, focus on using them in a way that aligns with your values and goals. Consider how your gifts can contribute to a greater good and use them to make a positive impact in the world.

For example, if you have a talent for music, consider performing at local charity events or teaching music to underprivileged youth. If you have a gift for leadership, consider using your skills to help advance a cause or organization that aligns with your values. By using your unique gifts in a meaningful way, you can cultivate a sense of fulfillment and purpose that goes beyond personal achievement.

It's important to note that embracing and using your unique gifts does not mean that you will never face challenges or obstacles. In fact, the road to fulfillment and happiness is often paved with setbacks and failures. However, by using your unique gifts and leaning into your strengths, you can develop the resilience and perseverance needed to overcome these challenges and come out stronger on the other side.

In conclusion, embracing and tapping into your unique gifts is an essential component of achieving ultimate happiness and fulfillment. By acknowledging and accepting your talents and strengths, seeking out opportunities to use them, and cultivating a sense of purpose and meaning through their application, you can unlock the secrets to a life filled with bliss. Remember, your unique gifts are what make you special and valuable, and they have the power to transform your life and the world around you.

28: Creating a Positive Environment: How to Create a Blissful Home and Work Environment

Introduction

The environment we live in plays a significant role in our lives. It has a direct impact on our mood, mental health, and overall well-being. We spend a considerable amount of time in our homes and workplaces, and therefore, it's important to ensure that these environments are conducive to our happiness and fulfillment. In this chapter, we will explore how to create a positive environment that fosters happiness, productivity, and fulfillment.

Part 1: Creating a Blissful Home Environment

Our homes are our sanctuaries; they are where we go to relax, unwind, and recharge. Creating a blissful home environment involves creating a space that is comfortable, inviting, and peaceful. Here are some tips for creating a blissful home environment:

Declutter and Organize

28: CREATING A POSITIVE ENVIRONMENT: HOW TO CREATE A BLISSFUL HOME AND WORK ENVIRONMENT

Clutter can cause stress and anxiety, so it's important to declutter and organize your home. Start by going through your belongings and getting rid of anything you no longer need or use. Next, organize your belongings in a way that makes sense and is easy to maintain. This will not only create a more serene and peaceful environment but will also save you time and energy in the long run.

Bring Nature Indoors

Nature has a calming effect on our minds and bodies. You can bring nature indoors by adding plants and flowers to your home. Plants not only add beauty to your home but also improve air quality and create a sense of calm and relaxation.

Create a Relaxing Space

Create a space in your home where you can relax and unwind. This could be a comfortable chair, a cozy reading nook, or a meditation corner. Make this space inviting by adding soft lighting, comfortable cushions, and anything else that helps you relax and destress.

28: CREATING A POSITIVE ENVIRONMENT: HOW TO CREATE A BLISSFUL HOME AND WORK ENVIRONMENT

Use Color Psychology

Colors have a powerful effect on our mood and emotions. Use color psychology to create a home environment that promotes happiness and calmness. For example, blue promotes calmness, green promotes relaxation, and yellow promotes happiness.

Let in Natural Light

Natural light has a positive effect on our mood and energy levels. Open up your curtains and blinds during the day to let in as much natural light as possible. This will create a bright and welcoming environment that promotes productivity and happiness.

Part 2: Creating a Blissful Work Environment

We spend a significant amount of time in our workplaces, and therefore, it's important to create a work environment that promotes productivity, creativity, and happiness. Here are some tips for creating a blissful work environment:

Organize Your Workspace

28: CREATING A POSITIVE ENVIRONMENT: HOW TO CREATE A BLISSFUL HOME AND WORK ENVIRONMENT

Just like at home, clutter can cause stress and anxiety in the workplace. Keep your workspace organized and tidy by getting rid of anything you don't need and keeping everything else in its proper place.

Personalize Your Workspace

Personalizing your workspace can make it feel more inviting and comfortable. Add photos of loved ones, inspirational quotes, and anything else that makes you feel happy and motivated.

Use Ergonomic Furniture

Sitting for long periods of time can cause physical discomfort and fatigue. Invest in ergonomic furniture, such as a comfortable chair and desk that are adjustable to your height, to reduce the risk of physical strain and promote productivity.

Let in Natural Light

Similar to at home, natural light has a positive effect on our mood and energy levels in the workplace. Try to position your workspace near a window or in a well-lit area to maximize natural light.

Create a Positive Atmosphere

A positive atmosphere can significantly impact our mood and productivity in the workplace. Surround yourself with positive coworkers and create a positive work environment by being kind and supportive to others.

Conclusion

Creating a positive environment at home and work is essential for our overall well-being and happiness. By following these tips, you can create a blissful home and work environment that promotes happiness, productivity, and fulfillment. Remember, small changes can make a big difference, so start by implementing one or two of these tips and build from there.

However, it's important to note that creating a positive environment isn't just about the physical space; it's also about your mindset and the energy you bring to that space. You can create a beautiful and comfortable home or workspace, but if your mindset is negative or stressed, you won't experience true bliss and fulfillment. So, in addition to creating a positive environment, focus on cultivating a positive mindset and bringing positive energy into your space.

In summary, creating a blissful environment involves decluttering and organizing, bringing nature indoors, creating a relaxing space, using color psychology, letting in natural light, personalizing your space, using ergonomic furniture, creating a positive atmosphere, and cultivating a positive mindset. By incorporating these tips into your home and work environments, you can create a space that fosters happiness, fulfillment, and well-being.

29: Simplifying Your Life: How to Simplify Your Life for Greater Joy and Fulfillment

In today's world, it is easy to get caught up in the hustle and bustle of everyday life. The constant demands on our time, energy, and attention can leave us feeling overwhelmed and stressed out. We may feel like we're always playing catch-up, never quite able to keep up with everything that's expected of us. However, there is a solution to this problem: simplifying our lives.

Simplifying your life is about streamlining your routines, minimizing your possessions, and focusing on what really matters to you. It's about decluttering your physical space and your mental space so that you can live a more intentional, purposeful life. In this chapter, we'll explore the benefits of simplifying your life and provide practical tips for doing so.

Why Simplify Your Life?

There are many benefits to simplifying your life. Here are just a few:

29: SIMPLIFYING YOUR LIFE: HOW TO SIMPLIFY YOUR LIFE FOR GREATER JOY AND FULFILLMENT

Reduced stress: When we have too much going on in our lives, it can be overwhelming. By simplifying our lives, we can reduce the amount of stress we experience on a daily basis.

Increased focus: When we have fewer distractions, we can focus more on the things that matter most to us. This can help us achieve our goals and live a more purposeful life.

More time: When we simplify our lives, we can free up more time for the things that are truly important to us, such as spending time with loved ones, pursuing our passions, or just relaxing.

Better health: Simplifying our lives can also improve our physical and mental health. When we're less stressed and have more time to take care of ourselves, we're more likely to be healthy and happy.

How to Simplify Your Life

Now that we've explored the benefits of simplifying your life, let's take a look at some practical tips for doing so.

Declutter your physical space: One of the easiest ways to

simplify your life is to declutter your physical space. This means getting rid of things you no longer need or use, organizing the things you do need, and creating a more minimalist living environment. Start small by decluttering one room at a time, and be honest with yourself about what you really need and what you can do without.

Streamline your routines: Another way to simplify your life is to streamline your daily routines. This might mean simplifying your morning routine by choosing your clothes the night before or preparing your breakfast in advance. It could also mean automating certain tasks, such as paying bills or scheduling appointments, so that you don't have to think about them as much.

Learn to say no: Saying no can be difficult, especially if you're a people pleaser. However, learning to say no to things that don't align with your values or priorities can be a powerful way to simplify your life. It can help you avoid overcommitting and feeling overwhelmed, and it can free up more time for the things that truly matter to you.

Focus on what matters: Simplifying your life is ultimately about focusing on what matters most to you. Take some time to reflect on your values and priorities, and think about how you can align your life with them. This might mean letting go of certain commitments or relationships, or it might mean pursuing a new hobby or career that aligns more closely with your values.

Practice mindfulness: Finally, practicing mindfulness can be a powerful way to simplify your life. Mindfulness is the practice of being present in the moment, without judgment. By practicing mindfulness, you can become more aware of your thoughts, feelings, and behaviors, and you can make more intentional choices about how you want to live your life.

Conclusion

Simplifying your life is not always easy, but it is well worth the effort. By decluttering your physical space, streamlining your routines, learning to say no, focusing on what matters, and practicing mindfulness, you can create a life that is more intentional, purposeful, and fulfilling. Remember, simplifying your life is not about depriving yourself or giving up things you love. It's about creating space for the things that truly matter to you and letting go of the things that don't.

As you begin to simplify your life, you may encounter resistance from others. Some people may not understand why you're making changes or may feel threatened by your newfound sense of clarity and purpose. It's important to remember that your life is your own, and you have the right to create the life you want. Don't let other people's opinions or expectations hold you back from living a life that brings you joy and fulfillment.

In conclusion, simplifying your life is an important step towards achieving bliss and unlocking the secrets to ultimate happiness and fulfillment. By decluttering your physical space, streamlining your routines, learning to say no, focusing on what matters, and practicing mindfulness, you can create a life that is more intentional, purposeful, and fulfilling. Remember, simplifying your life is a journey, not a destination. Take it one step at a time, and enjoy the process of creating a life that truly brings you joy and happiness.

30: Practicing Mindful Consumption: How to Live a Sustainable and Mindful Lifestyle for Bliss

Introduction:

In today's fast-paced world, it's easy to get caught up in the hustle and bustle of life. We're constantly bombarded with information, advertisements, and social media notifications, leaving us feeling overwhelmed, stressed, and disconnected from ourselves and the world around us. But what if there was a way to slow down, tune in, and live a more sustainable and mindful lifestyle? In this chapter, we'll explore the concept of mindful consumption and how it can help us achieve ultimate happiness and fulfillment.

What is Mindful Consumption?

Mindful consumption is the practice of being aware and intentional about the things we buy, use, and consume. It involves taking a step back from the constant cycle of consumption and asking ourselves if what we're buying or using aligns with our values and goals. It's about being mindful of our impact on the environment, on our own well-being, and on the well-being of others.

30: PRACTICING MINDFUL CONSUMPTION: HOW TO LIVE A SUSTAINABLE AND MINDFUL LIFESTYLE FOR BLISS

Why is Mindful Consumption Important?

Mindful consumption is important for several reasons. First and foremost, it allows us to make more conscious and informed choices about the products we buy and the companies we support. By choosing to support ethical and sustainable brands, we can have a positive impact on the environment, on workers' rights, and on our own health and well-being.

Additionally, practicing mindful consumption can help us save money and reduce clutter. By being more intentional about what we buy, we can avoid impulse purchases and only bring items into our homes that truly serve a purpose and bring us joy. This can lead to a more minimalist and clutter-free lifestyle, which can in turn reduce stress and increase feelings of peace and contentment.

How to Practice Mindful Consumption:

Practicing mindful consumption is all about being intentional and aware of our choices. Here are some tips for incorporating mindful consumption into your daily life:

30: PRACTICING MINDFUL CONSUMPTION: HOW TO LIVE A SUSTAINABLE AND MINDFUL LIFESTYLE FOR BLISS

Define your values and goals: Before making any purchases, take a moment to reflect on your values and goals. What's important to you? What do you want to achieve? By having a clear sense of your priorities, you can make more informed choices about what to buy and use.

Do your research: Before buying a product, take the time to research the company and its practices. Look for brands that align with your values and support ethical and sustainable practices. There are also several apps and websites that can help you find ethical and sustainable products, such as Good On You and Ethical Consumer.

Practice the 30-day rule: Before making an impulse purchase, wait 30 days. This can help you avoid buying things you don't really need or want and can give you time to reflect on whether the purchase aligns with your values and goals.

Buy used or secondhand: Buying used or secondhand items is a great way to reduce waste and save money. There are several online marketplaces for buying and selling used goods, such as ThredUp and Poshmark.

30: PRACTICING MINDFUL CONSUMPTION: HOW TO LIVE A SUSTAINABLE AND MINDFUL LIFESTYLE FOR BLISS

Choose quality over quantity: Instead of buying a lot of cheap, low-quality items, invest in a few high-quality items that will last longer and bring you more joy. This can help you save money in the long run and reduce waste.

Practice gratitude: Instead of constantly seeking more and more, take time to appreciate what you already have. Practicing gratitude can help shift your focus from what you don't have to what you do have, which can lead to feelings of contentment and happiness.

Conclusion:

Practicing mindful consumption is a powerful tool for achieving ultimate happiness and fulfillment. By being intentional and aware of our choices, we can align our consumption habits with our values and goals, reduce waste, save money, and increase feelings of contentment and peace. Whether you're just starting out on your mindful consumption journey or you're a seasoned practitioner, remember that it's a process, not a destination. There will be times when you slip up or make choices that don't align with your values, and that's okay. The important thing is to keep moving forward and making progress towards a more sustainable and mindful lifestyle.

In addition to the tips outlined above, there are several other practices that can help you cultivate a more mindful and sustainable lifestyle, such as:

Mindful eating: Paying attention to what and how you eat can help you make more conscious and healthy choices. Try to eat slowly and without distractions, savoring each bite and tuning in to your body's hunger and fullness cues.

Mindful technology use: Being mindful of how much time you spend on your phone or computer can help you reduce stress and increase feelings of connectedness. Try setting boundaries around technology use, such as not using your phone during meals or before bedtime.

Mindful travel: When traveling, try to be mindful of your impact on the environment and local communities. Choose eco-friendly transportation options and support local businesses and cultural experiences.

Mindful relationships: Being mindful in your relationships

can help you cultivate deeper connections and increase feelings of happiness and fulfillment. Practice active listening, empathy, and kindness in your interactions with others.

Remember, practicing mindful consumption is not just about what you buy or use, but also about how you live your life. By incorporating mindfulness into all aspects of your life, you can cultivate a more sustainable and fulfilling lifestyle that aligns with your values and goals.

In conclusion, practicing mindful consumption is a powerful tool for achieving ultimate happiness and fulfillment. By being intentional and aware of our choices, we can align our consumption habits with our values and goals, reduce waste, save money, and increase feelings of contentment and peace. Whether you're just starting out on your mindful consumption journey or you're a seasoned practitioner, remember to be patient, compassionate, and persistent in your efforts to live a more sustainable and mindful lifestyle.

31: Giving Back: The Role of Giving and Service in a Blissful Life

Bliss is not just a state of mind, it's a way of life. It's about cultivating a sense of joy and fulfillment in every aspect of your life, from your relationships to your career to your personal growth. And one of the most important aspects of a blissful life is giving back to others.

When we give back to others, we not only help those in need, but we also enrich our own lives. Giving back can bring us a sense of purpose, meaning, and connection that is essential for a truly blissful life.

In this chapter, we'll explore the role of giving and service in a blissful life. We'll look at the benefits of giving back, the different ways you can give, and how to make giving a regular part of your life. So let's dive in!

The Benefits of Giving Back

There are many benefits to giving back, both for the recipient and the giver. Here are just a few of them:

A Sense of Purpose and Meaning - Giving back can help us find a sense of purpose and meaning in our lives. When we know that we're making a positive impact on the world, it can give us a sense of fulfillment and satisfaction that is hard to find elsewhere.

Increased Happiness - Giving back can actually make us happier. Studies have shown that when we give to others, it activates the pleasure centers in our brains, leading to a "helper's high" that can elevate our mood and increase our overall happiness.

Improved Health - Giving back has also been linked to improved physical health. Studies have shown that people who volunteer regularly have lower levels of stress and a lower risk of depression and heart disease.

Enhanced Relationships - Giving back can also strengthen our relationships with others. When we work together on a common goal, it can deepen our connections and help us feel more connected to our communities.

The Different Ways You Can Give

There are many different ways to give back, and the best way for you will depend on your interests, skills, and resources. Here are just a few of the ways you can give:

Volunteer - Volunteering your time and energy is one of the most direct ways to give back. There are countless organizations and causes that rely on volunteers, so find one that aligns with your values and interests and start giving your time.

Donate Money - If you don't have a lot of time to volunteer, you can still make a difference by donating money to a worthy cause. There are many organizations doing important work around the world, so find one that resonates with you and make a contribution.

Share Your Skills - If you have a particular skill or talent, consider sharing it with others. Whether it's teaching a class, mentoring a young person, or offering pro bono services to a nonprofit, your skills can be a valuable resource for those in need.

Practice Random Acts of Kindness - You don't need to join an organization or donate money to make a difference. Small acts of kindness, such as buying someone a cup of coffee or helping a stranger with their groceries, can make a big impact on someone's day.

Making Giving a Regular Part of Your Life

Giving back doesn't have to be a one-time event or occasional activity. To truly experience the benefits of giving, it's important to make it a regular part of your life. Here are some tips for doing so:

Find a Cause You're Passionate About - Giving back is most fulfilling when it's aligned with our passions and values. So find a cause or organization that you truly care about and make it a priority in your life.

Set Realistic Goals - Giving back can be overwhelming if you try to do too much at once. Instead, set realistic goals for yourself. Start small and build up over time as you become more comfortable and confident in your giving.

Incorporate Giving into Your Routine - Make giving a regular part of your routine. Whether it's volunteering once a week, making a monthly donation to a cause you care about, or performing random acts of kindness daily, find a way to incorporate giving into your daily or weekly routine.

31: GIVING BACK: THE ROLE OF GIVING AND SERVICE IN A BLISSFUL LIFE

Get Involved in Your Community - Getting involved in your community is a great way to give back and connect with others. Attend community events, join a local organization, or simply volunteer at a local food bank or shelter.

Encourage Others to Give - Giving back is contagious. Encourage your friends, family, and coworkers to get involved in giving back, and you'll create a ripple effect of kindness and positivity in your community.

Conclusion

Giving back is an essential part of a blissful life. When we give to others, we not only help those in need, but we also enrich our own lives. Giving back can bring us a sense of purpose, meaning, and connection that is essential for a truly blissful life.

Whether you choose to volunteer your time, donate money, share your skills, or perform random acts of kindness, there are countless ways to give back and make a positive impact on the world. And by making giving a regular part of your life, you'll experience the many benefits of giving and help create a happier, more connected, and more blissful world.

32: Living in the Present Moment: The Power of Living in the Now for Greater Bliss

We live in a world that is constantly moving, changing, and evolving. With the advancement of technology, we have become accustomed to instant gratification, and we are constantly bombarded with information, distractions, and tasks that demand our attention. As a result, it can be challenging to stay present and enjoy the current moment fully.

Living in the present moment is the art of being fully aware of what is happening right now. It involves experiencing life as it unfolds and embracing each moment with all its beauty, wonder, and challenges. When we are present, we are fully engaged in the present moment, free from the regrets of the past or the worries of the future. We are centered, calm, and content, and we can tap into a deep sense of peace and joy.

Living in the present moment is a skill that takes practice and patience. It requires us to let go of our ego, expectations, and judgments, and cultivate a deep sense of self-awareness and mindfulness. Here are some tips on how to

live in the present moment and experience greater bliss in
your life:

Practice mindfulness: Mindfulness is the practice of being
fully present and engaged in the current moment. It involves paying attention to your thoughts, feelings, and surroundings without judgment. Mindfulness can be practiced
through meditation, yoga, or simply taking a few minutes
each day to focus on your breath and observe your thoughts.
By practicing mindfulness, you can become more aware of
your thoughts and emotions and learn to let go of negative
patterns that may be holding you back from living in the
present moment.

Embrace your senses: One of the best ways to stay present
is to engage your senses fully. Take time to notice the sights,
sounds, smells, tastes, and textures of your environment. Be
fully present in the experience and allow yourself to be im-
mersed in the moment. This can be as simple as savoring
your morning coffee or taking a walk in nature and paying
attention to the sounds of the birds and the rustling of the
leaves.

Let go of the past: One of the biggest obstacles to living in the present moment is holding onto regrets and grudges from the past. It's essential to acknowledge your past experiences and learn from them, but it's equally important to let go of them and move on. Holding onto negative emotions from the past only robs you of the joy and potential of the present moment.

Release worry about the future: Similarly, worrying about the future can also prevent us from fully experiencing the present moment. While it's natural to have concerns about the future, it's important to focus on the present and take action towards your goals in the moment. Recognize that the future is unpredictable, and the best way to prepare for it is to focus on what you can control right now.

Practice gratitude: Gratitude is the practice of acknowledging and appreciating the good things in your life. By focusing on what you have rather than what you lack, you can cultivate a sense of contentment and fulfillment in the present moment. Take time each day to reflect on the things you are grateful for, whether it's a loving relationship, a fulfilling job, or a beautiful sunset.

Connect with others: Finally, one of the best ways to experience greater bliss in the present moment is to connect with others. Whether it's through meaningful conversations, shared experiences, or acts of kindness, human connection can bring joy, purpose, and fulfillment into your life. Make an effort to cultivate meaningful relationships with the people around you and take time to appreciate the moments you share together.

Living in the present moment is a powerful tool for achieving greater happiness, fulfillment, and purpose in your life. By practicing mindfulness, embracing your senses, letting go of the past and future, cultivating gratitude, and connecting with others, you can experience the richness and beauty of life in a profound way.

However, living in the present moment can be easier said than done. We often find ourselves distracted by our thoughts, worries, and external stimuli, which can prevent us from fully engaging with the present moment. It's important to remember that living in the present moment is a practice that requires patience, persistence, and self-compassion. Here are some additional tips on how to cultivate the art of present moment living:

Practice self-compassion: Living in the present moment can be challenging, especially when we are dealing with stress, anxiety, or difficult emotions. It's important to practice self-compassion and be gentle with ourselves when we are struggling. Instead of judging ourselves for not being fully present, we can acknowledge our thoughts and feelings with kindness and curiosity, and use them as an opportunity to deepen our awareness.

Set reminders: It can be helpful to set reminders throughout the day to bring yourself back to the present moment. This could be a simple alarm on your phone or a post-it note on your computer screen. When the reminder goes off, take a few deep breaths and focus on the present moment, even if it's just for a few seconds.

Incorporate mindfulness into your daily routine: To make living in the present moment a habit, it can be helpful to incorporate mindfulness into your daily routine. This could be as simple as taking a few mindful breaths before starting your workday or practicing mindful eating during your lunch break. By making mindfulness a part of your daily routine, you can develop a greater sense of presence and awareness throughout your day.

Take a digital detox: Our devices and technology can be a major source of distraction, preventing us from fully engaging with the present moment. Consider taking a digital detox and unplugging from your devices for a certain amount of time each day. This can help you reconnect with the world around you and cultivate a deeper sense of presence and connection.

Engage in activities that bring you joy: Living in the present moment is not just about being mindful and aware. It's also about experiencing joy, pleasure, and fulfillment in the current moment. Take time to engage in activities that bring you joy and make you feel fully alive, whether it's spending time in nature, pursuing a creative hobby, or spending quality time with loved ones.

In conclusion, living in the present moment is a powerful tool for achieving greater bliss and fulfillment in every aspect of your life. By practicing mindfulness, embracing your senses, letting go of the past and future, cultivating gratitude, connecting with others, and incorporating these practices into your daily routine, you can experience the richness and beauty of life in a profound way. Remember, the present moment is the only moment that truly exists. Embrace it fully, and you will unlock the secrets to ultimate happiness and fulfillment.

33: Mindful Technology Use: How to Use Technology Mindfully for a Blissful Life

Technology has become an integral part of our lives, and it's hard to imagine a day without it. We use technology for communication, entertainment, work, and many other aspects of our lives. While technology has made our lives easier in many ways, it has also brought with it some negative consequences, such as addiction, distraction, and anxiety. However, if used mindfully, technology can be a tool for achieving bliss and fulfillment in our lives. In this chapter, we'll explore how to use technology mindfully for a blissful life.

The Negative Impact of Technology

Before we dive into how to use technology mindfully, let's take a look at the negative impact of technology on our lives. One of the biggest problems with technology is addiction. We're addicted to our smartphones, social media, and other online platforms. We can't seem to put our phones down, even when we're with friends or family. This addiction can lead to distraction, anxiety, and a lack of focus.

Another negative impact of technology is the constant bombardment of information. We're constantly bombarded with news, notifications, and messages, which can lead to information overload and a feeling of overwhelm. We're also more connected than ever, but we're often not truly connecting with others. We're more likely to communicate through screens than face-to-face, which can lead to feelings of loneliness and isolation.

The Importance of Mindful Technology Use

Given the negative impact of technology on our lives, it's important to use technology mindfully. Mindful technology use means using technology intentionally, with awareness, and with a clear purpose. It means using technology as a tool for achieving our goals, rather than letting it control us.

Mindful technology use has many benefits. It can help us be more productive, reduce our stress levels, and improve our relationships. It can also help us cultivate a sense of presence and mindfulness in our lives.

How to Use Technology Mindfully

33: MINDFUL TECHNOLOGY USE: HOW TO USE TECH-NOLOGY MINDFULLY FOR A BLISSFUL LIFE

Now let's explore how to use technology mindfully for a blissful life.

Set Intentions

The first step to using technology mindfully is to set intentions. Before using your phone or computer, take a moment to think about your intention. What do you want to accomplish? Are you using technology to connect with friends or family? Are you using it to get work done? Having a clear intention can help you use technology more intentionally and with purpose.

Practice Mindful Breathing

Before using technology, take a few deep breaths to center yourself. Focus on your breath and bring your attention to the present moment. This can help you cultivate a sense of presence and mindfulness, which can help you use technology more intentionally.

Create Boundaries

Create boundaries around your technology use. For example, you could turn off notifications during certain times of the day or limit your social media use to certain times. Setting boundaries can help you use technology more intentionally and reduce distraction.

Use Technology to Enhance Relationships

Instead of using technology to replace face-to-face communication, use it to enhance relationships. For example, you could use video chat to connect with friends or family who live far away. You could also use social media to stay in touch with friends or family who you don't see often.

Take Breaks

Take breaks from technology throughout the day. Go for a walk, read a book, or do something else that doesn't involve technology. Taking breaks can help you reduce your stress levels and improve your overall well-being.

Practice Gratitude

Finally, practice gratitude for the technology in your life. Technology has made our lives easier in many ways, and it's important to appreciate the benefits it brings. By practicing gratitude, you can cultivate a sense of appreciation and contentment in your life.

Conclusion

In conclusion, mindful technology use can be a powerful tool for achieving bliss and fulfillment in our lives. By setting intentions, practicing mindful breathing, creating boundaries, using technology to enhance relationships, taking breaks, and practicing gratitude, we can use technology more intentionally and with purpose. When we use technology mindfully, we can reduce our stress levels, improve our relationships, and cultivate a sense of presence and mindfulness in our lives.

However, mindful technology use is just one aspect of achieving bliss and fulfillment in our lives. To truly experience a blissful life, we must also cultivate meaningful relationships, find purpose and meaning in our lives, and take care of our physical and mental health. By taking a holistic approach to our well-being, we can create a life that is filled with joy, meaning, and purpose.

In this book, we'll explore all of the aspects of achieving bliss and fulfillment in our lives. From mastering our mindset to cultivating meaningful relationships and creating a purposeful life, we'll provide you with the tools and strategies you need to create a life that is filled with happiness, fulfillment, and joy.

Remember, achieving bliss and fulfillment is a journey, not a destination. It requires effort, commitment, and a willingness to embrace change. But with the right mindset and strategies, you can create a life that is filled with happiness, joy, and purpose. So, let's embark on this journey together and discover the secrets to ultimate happiness and fulfillment!

34: The Importance of Rest and Relaxation: How to Incorporate Rest and Relaxation into Your Life for Bliss

Rest and relaxation are two crucial components in achieving a blissful life. Many of us lead busy and stressful lives, leaving little time for ourselves. We constantly try to juggle multiple tasks and responsibilities, leaving us feeling drained and overwhelmed. It is essential to incorporate rest and relaxation into our daily routine to maintain a healthy mind and body. In this chapter, we will explore the significance of rest and relaxation and learn how to incorporate it into our daily lives to achieve ultimate happiness and fulfillment.

The Importance of Rest

Rest is an essential component of our daily routine. It is crucial for our physical and mental well-being. When we sleep, our body goes through a rejuvenating process that helps repair and regenerate our cells. Adequate sleep is essential for optimal brain function, concentration, and memory. It also helps regulate our hormones, leading to better overall health and vitality.

34: THE IMPORTANCE OF REST AND RELAXATION: HOW TO INCORPORATE REST AND RELAXATION INTO YOUR LIFE FOR BLISS

Unfortunately, many of us do not get enough rest due to busy schedules or poor sleep habits. Lack of sleep can have detrimental effects on our physical and mental health. Chronic sleep deprivation can lead to a weakened immune system, weight gain, depression, and anxiety.

It is essential to prioritize rest and make it a part of our daily routine. To get optimal rest, we should aim for seven to eight hours of sleep every night. We should also establish a consistent sleep schedule, avoid caffeine and alcohol before bedtime, and create a comfortable sleep environment.

The Importance of Relaxation

Relaxation is another critical component of achieving a blissful life. When we relax, we reduce stress and tension, leading to better overall health and well-being. Relaxation can also boost our creativity and productivity, leading to increased motivation and fulfillment.

Unfortunately, many of us struggle to relax due to busy schedules or an inability to disconnect from work and technology. The constant stimulation and pressure to be productive can lead to burnout, fatigue, and decreased overall happiness.

It is crucial to prioritize relaxation and make it a part of our daily routine. We should aim to take regular breaks throughout the day, engage in activities that bring us joy and relaxation, and disconnect from technology and work during our free time.

Incorporating Rest and Relaxation into Your Life

Now that we understand the importance of rest and relaxation, let's explore how to incorporate it into our daily lives. Here are some tips to help you prioritize rest and relaxation:

Establish a consistent sleep schedule - Aim to go to bed and wake up at the same time every day, even on weekends.

Create a comfortable sleep environment - Ensure that your bedroom is conducive to sleep by keeping it dark, cool, and quiet. Invest in a comfortable mattress and pillows.

Avoid caffeine and alcohol before bedtime - Both caffeine

and alcohol can interfere with your sleep quality, leading to decreased restfulness and overall health.

Take regular breaks throughout the day - Take a five-minute break every hour to stretch, take a walk, or simply close your eyes and breathe.

Engage in activities that bring you joy and relaxation - Whether it's reading a book, practicing yoga, or taking a bubble bath, make time for activities that bring you joy and relaxation.

Disconnect from technology and work during your free time - Set boundaries around your work and technology use, and allow yourself time to disconnect and recharge.

By incorporating rest and relaxation into your daily routine, you will experience increased overall happiness and fulfillment. Prioritizing your physical and mental well-being is the first step in achieving ultimate bliss in every aspect of your life.

35: Overcoming Adversity: How to Turn Adversity into Opportunity for Greater Bliss

Adversity is an inevitable part of life. At some point or another, we all face challenges, setbacks, and obstacles that threaten to derail our progress and dampen our spirits. But how we respond to adversity is what separates those who thrive from those who simply survive. In this chapter, we'll explore the key strategies and mindset shifts you can use to overcome adversity and transform it into an opportunity for greater happiness and fulfillment.

Embrace the Challenge

The first step in turning adversity into an opportunity is to embrace the challenge. Rather than seeing setbacks and obstacles as insurmountable roadblocks, view them as opportunities to grow, learn, and improve. The truth is that challenges often present us with the chance to develop new skills, strengthen our resolve, and push past our limits. When faced with adversity, take a moment to step back and assess the situation objectively. Ask yourself: what can I learn from this? How can I grow and become a better person as a result of this challenge? By embracing the challenge, you'll be better equipped to navigate it with grace and resilience.

Cultivate Resilience

Resilience is the ability to bounce back from setbacks and overcome adversity. It's a key trait that separates those who thrive from those who struggle in the face of challenges. To cultivate resilience, start by adopting a growth mindset. This means viewing setbacks as temporary and believing that you have the power to overcome them. Practice self-compassion and self-care, and surround yourself with a supportive network of friends and family. When faced with adversity, focus on your strengths and the things you can control, and take small, positive steps forward. Over time, these actions will help you build resilience and overcome even the most difficult challenges.

Practice Gratitude

Gratitude is a powerful tool for overcoming adversity. When we focus on what we're grateful for, we shift our attention away from our problems and towards the things that bring us joy and fulfillment. This doesn't mean ignoring the challenges we face, but rather reframing our perspective to see the good in every situation. Take time each day to reflect on the things you're grateful for, whether it's a supportive friend, a warm cup of coffee, or a beautiful sunset. By cultivating gratitude, you'll build a stronger sense of resilience and find it easier to overcome adversity.

Develop a Growth Mindset

A growth mindset is the belief that our abilities and intelligence can be developed through hard work, dedication, and learning. Those with a growth mindset see challenges as opportunities for growth and are more likely to persevere in the face of adversity. To develop a growth mindset, focus on the process rather than the outcome. Embrace challenges as opportunities to learn and grow, and approach them with curiosity and a willingness to experiment. Celebrate your progress along the way, and use setbacks as opportunities to refine your approach and try again.

Build a Support Network

Finally, building a strong support network is key to overcoming adversity. When faced with challenges, it's natural to feel alone and overwhelmed. But having a network of supportive friends, family members, or mentors can make all the difference. Seek out people who share your values and goals, and who will support and encourage you through difficult times. Remember that asking for help is a sign of strength, not weakness. By building a strong support network, you'll have the resources you need to overcome adversity and achieve greater happiness and fulfillment.

In conclusion, adversity is a natural part of life, but it doesn't have to be a source of despair. By embracing the challenge, cultivating resilience, practicing gratitude, developing a growth mindset, and building a support network, you can turn adversity into an opportunity for growth and greater happiness and fulfillment. Remember that the most successful and fulfilled people are not those who have never faced adversity, but rather those who have learned to overcome it and emerge stronger as a result.

It's important to recognize that overcoming adversity is not a one-time event, but a lifelong process. Life is full of ups and downs, and challenges will continue to arise no matter how much we prepare. The key is to approach each challenge with a growth mindset, embracing it as an opportunity to learn and grow.

In addition to the strategies discussed above, there are a few other tips that can help you overcome adversity:

Practice self-compassion: Be kind and compassionate to yourself, especially when things don't go as planned. Recognize that setbacks and failures are a normal part of the human experience, and that you are not alone in your struggles.

Focus on what you can control: When faced with adversity, it's easy to feel helpless and overwhelmed. To regain a sense of control, focus on the things that are within your power to change. This may include your attitude, your approach, or your actions.

Take care of your physical health: Our physical health and mental health are deeply intertwined. When we take care of our bodies, we are better equipped to handle stress and adversity. Make sure to eat a healthy diet, get enough sleep, and engage in regular exercise.

35: OVERCOMING ADVERSITY: HOW TO TURN AD-VERSITY INTO OPPORTUNITY FOR GREATER BLISS

Find meaning and purpose: Adversity can often shake our sense of purpose and leave us feeling lost or directionless. To combat this, focus on the things that bring you meaning and fulfillment, whether it's your family, your career, or your hobbies.

By following these tips and strategies, you can develop the resilience and mindset needed to overcome adversity and achieve greater happiness and fulfillment in every aspect of your life.

In summary, overcoming adversity is a challenging but essential part of the human experience. By embracing the challenge, cultivating resilience, practicing gratitude, developing a growth mindset, building a support network, and taking care of our physical and mental health, we can turn adversity into an opportunity for growth and greater happiness and fulfillment. Remember that with the right mindset and tools, you can overcome any obstacle that comes your way.

36: Conclusion: The Journey to Ultimate Happiness and Fulfillment

As we come to the end of this comprehensive guide to achieving bliss in every aspect of your life, I want to take a moment to reflect on the journey we've taken together. We've explored the many different ways in which we can cultivate happiness and fulfillment in our lives, from mastering our mindset to cultivating meaningful relationships and creating a purposeful life. Along the way, we've learned that there are no shortcuts to true happiness and that the journey to bliss is a lifelong process.

One of the key takeaways from this guide is the importance of mastering our mindset. We've learned that our thoughts have a powerful impact on our emotions, behaviors, and ultimately, our life experiences. By learning to cultivate a positive mindset, we can transform our lives and create a more joyful and fulfilling existence. We've explored a range of different strategies for doing this, from practicing gratitude to reframing negative self-talk and cultivating self-compassion.

We've also delved into the importance of cultivating meaningful relationships in our lives. Humans are social
creatures, and we thrive when we are connected to others in
positive and fulfilling ways. Whether it's through family,
friendships, romantic partnerships, or community involve-
ment, we've learned that nurturing these connections can
have a profound impact on our overall well-being.

In addition to our relationships, we've explored the importance of finding purpose and meaning in our lives. When we
have a sense of direction and a feeling that our actions are
contributing to something greater than ourselves, we are
more likely to experience a deep sense of fulfillment and
satisfaction. We've looked at ways to identify our personal
values, align our actions with those values, and create a
sense of purpose in our daily lives.

Throughout this guide, we've also acknowledged that the
journey to bliss is not without its challenges. We've explored
the importance of resilience, self-care, and self-compassion
in navigating the inevitable bumps in the road. We've
learned that setbacks and struggles are a natural part of the
human experience, and that it's our response to those chal-

lenges that ultimately determines our level of happiness and fulfillment.

As we wrap up this guide, I want to emphasize that achieving ultimate happiness and fulfillment is not a destination that we can simply arrive at and stay put. It's a lifelong journey that requires ongoing attention, care, and effort. It's a process of continual growth, learning, and evolution, and it requires us to stay open and curious to the world around us.

So, as you continue on your journey towards ultimate happiness and fulfillment, remember to stay focused on the present moment, embrace the inevitable ups and downs of life, and never stop seeking out new opportunities for growth and learning. Remember that true bliss is not something that can be found outside of ourselves, but rather something that we must cultivate within ourselves.

With this guide as your roadmap, I have no doubt that you will continue to make great strides towards living your most joyful and fulfilling life. Remember to be kind to yourself, be patient with the process, and most importantly, enjoy the journey. The road to bliss may not always be easy, but it is always worth it.

Thank You

As we reach the end of this book, I want to say thanks for reading this book.

I want to get this information out to as many people as possible. If you found this book helpful, I would greatly appreciate you leaving me a review. This helps others find the book as well.

Disclaimer

This document is geared towards providing exact and reliable information in regards to the topic and issue covered. The publication is sold on the idea that the publisher is not required to render an accounting, officially permitted, or otherwise, qualified services. If advice is necessary, legal, financial, medical or professional, a practiced individual in the profession should be ordered.

This information is not presented by a financial or medical practitioner and is for entertainment, educational and informational purposes only. The content is not intended as a substitute for professional medical advice, diagnosis, or treatment. Always seek the advice of your physician or other qualified health care provider with any questions you may have regarding a medical condition. Never disregard professional medical advice or delay in seeking it because of something you have read.

The information provided herein is stated to be truthful and consistent, in that any liability, in terms of inattention or otherwise, by any usage or abuse of any policies, processes, or directions contained within is the solitary and utter responsibility of the recipient reader. Under no circumstances

DISCLAIMER

will any legal responsibility or blame be held against the publisher for any reparation, damages, or monetary loss due to the information herein, either directly or indirectly.